The People Who Run Law Firms

Lessons Learned from Law Firm Leaders

Editor
Bill Knight

Managing director
Sian O'Neill

The People Who Run Law Firms: Lessons Learned from Law Firm Leaders
is published by

Globe Law and Business Ltd
3 Mylor Close
Horsell
Woking
Surrey GU21 4DD
United Kingdom
Tel: +44 20 3745 4770
www.globelawandbusiness.com

Printed and bound by CPI Group (UK) Ltd, Croydon, CR0 4YY

The People Who Run Law Firms: Lessons Learned from Law Firm Leaders

ISBN 9781787424623
EPUB ISBN 9781787424630
Adobe PDF ISBN 9781787424647
Mobi ISBN 9781787424654

Table of contents

Foreword, Bill Knight Editor 5

I. Olayemi Anyanechi Founder and managing partner, Sefton Fross 8

II. Edward Braham Former senior partner, Freshfields Bruckhaus Deringer LLP 16

III. Melissa Butler London office executive partner, White & Case LLP 26

IV. Michael Chissick Managing partner, Fieldfisher LLP 36

V. Rafael Fontana Senior partner, Cuatrecasas 46

VI. James Palmer Former chair and senior partner, Herbert Smith Freehills 54

VII. Kathleen Russ Senior partner, Travers Smith LLP 64

VIII. Victoria Sampson and Joseph Oates Partners, CooperBurnett LLP 76

IX. Aku Sorainen Founder and senior partner, Sorainen 86

X. Linda Woolley Managing partner, Kingsley Napley LLP 96

About the editor 106

About Globe Law and Business 108

Foreword

Bill Knight
Editor

The legal education sharpens the mind by narrowing it. When a lawyer is asked to take the helm of the ship and leave the safe harbour of their legal practice, they are likely to be starting a voyage to a destination well outside their comfort zone. After his first day in office, President Truman is reported to have said that he felt as if a bale of hay had landed on him. As a former senior partner, I know what he meant.

Some of those interviewed in this Special Report are senior partners and others are managing partners. The roles change from firm to firm, but there are common characteristics. Senior partners are ambassadors for their firm and responsible for the well-being of the partnership. With the exception of those who have founded their own firm, they tend to be moving towards the end of their legal careers. Managing partners run the firm day to day and are typically younger. Senior partners often continue to do some client work, while partners managing an entire firm do not. The common thread is that senior and managing partners have accepted responsibilities beyond their legal practice and have had to learn new skills and unlearn some old ways of thinking.

As Linda Woolley, the managing partner of Kingsley Napley says, the move to managing the firm can be a poisoned chalice. At the end of

"The law firm leader will face a highly educated and clever audience who have been trained to find fault – to point out risk rather than benefit – but who are often themselves insecure and in need of reassurance."

your term you can lose your practice, and you're not a professional manager either, so you have nowhere else to go.

And what about the people? The law firm leader will face a highly educated and clever audience who have been trained to find fault – to point out risk rather than benefit – but who are often themselves insecure and in need of reassurance.

So why would any lawyer want to do this job? The irony is that most agree that only a lawyer, and a good one at that, is qualified. Only a lawyer knows what it is like to be a lawyer. Only a lawyer is likely to be listened to by his or her partners. Only a lawyer can command the necessary respect.

I thought it was time that we heard from the men and women running law firms about their careers, the challenges they face and their ambitions. I found them to be surprisingly cheerful. They had all been successful lawyers, but many of them said that this was the most rewarding time of their careers. The reason for that, I would like to suggest, is that they are changing and developing. As WB Yeats said: "Happiness is neither virtue, nor pleasure, nor this thing, nor that, but growth. We are happy when we are growing."

The men and women interviewed for this report come from a variety of backgrounds and a variety of firms in the UK and abroad. None of them had any significant management training. They may have read a few books, or been on a short course, but their real training has been in the law and the practice of the law. Lawyers are suspicious by nature and, as a rule, they are suspicious of management consultants, but they are happy to take advice on specialist issues.

There are some common themes. Many of those interviewed advised future senior or managing partners that they should not be afraid to make mistakes, but to learn from them. As a lawyer, of course, you are not allowed to make a mistake. If you do, then you might have to notify the insurers. But as a business leader you can, indeed you should, calculate the consequences of failure and take risks. That is a major change.

Most of them said how important it is to value the business functions within the firm, such as finance, IT, and human resources, and to involve them at the top level. These functions are underappreciated by partners who do not have management responsibilities.

They all agreed on the need to listen, but they are all leaders: when it comes down to it, their most important function is to lead – to take decisions, sometimes against stiff opposition. This is the most difficult aspect of their job.

This Special Report was written in the shadow of COVID-19. Most of those interviewed had been apprehensive about the effect of the pandemic at its outset but had been pleasantly surprised by the way business held up. Indeed, some said that, with restricted expenses, 2020/21 was going to be a good year financially. It was too soon to predict the long-term impact on legal practice.

I found these leaders to be a very effective group of people – highly intelligent, very hardworking and committed, and as modest as their positions allow. I hope you enjoy hearing what they have to say.

April 2021

Olayemi Anyanechi

Founder and managing partner, Sefton Fross

Olayemi Anyanechi is the founder and managing partner of Sefton Fross, a full-service law firm in Lagos, Nigeria, with 11 lawyers practising in finance, energy and corporate and commercial law. Nigeria has a burgeoning legal market but the majority of its 70,000 practising lawyers are sole practitioners. There are a few larger firms but most firms have fewer than six lawyers and specialise in only one or two areas of law.

Early years

Olayemi was good at science when she was growing up in Nigeria and while her parents wanted her to be a doctor, it was never the job for her. Unable to stand the sight of blood, she also found the whole idea of being a doctor emotionally exhausting: "I've seen *Love Story* twenty times and I still cry like a baby."

So when she went to the University of Ibadan she studied chemistry, but it proved to be a disappointment – it wasn't "real" enough for her. "I knew that Fortran was a dead language," she says, referring to the original scientific computing language. She changed direction to study law because it was all about "real people, real experience, in real time".

First jobs

Olayemi's first job was at a Nigerian bank but her boss advised her that she was not being challenged enough and advised her to go back to law. So, in 2002, by this time a mother of two, she set off to study for her master's degree at Wolfson College, Cambridge, something which was only possible with the support of her family. Then, after a three-month internship in the Inner Temple (UK), she returned to Lagos to work for Olaniwun Ajayi LP (OALP), one of Nigeria's leading firms. Olayemi cannot remember her first day in the office, but she relates a story about something that happened a few weeks later, something that she will never forget:

> *The firm was a competitive place and they wanted to see what this supposedly smart lady from Cambridge could do. One day I was talking to two of the partners and one younger associate – one of their astute lawyers – and they asked me a question. I told them I didn't know the answer, so they asked me more questions and although I knew a lot of the answers, I refused to play their game and kept saying "I don't know".*
>
> *They said, "So you don't know all these things ... didn't you just come from Cambridge?" to which I replied, "OK, let me ask you some questions". So I quizzed one of the lawyers, and he didn't know all the answers either.*
>
> *I told them: "You see – I don't know everything, but neither do you."*

When asked if the lawyers asking her questions were men, Olayemi said that they were. But the point, she explains, was that she was not going to pretend to be something that she was not. She was comfortable in her own skin.

Her work at OALP centred mainly around banking and finance and she was soon involved in major transactions. Olayemi tells me that OALP was a great firm with great work, and that her "wonderful experience" there gave her a solid foundation in the law. Olayemi says that lawyers today can research a problem simply by turning to Google or *Practical Law*, whereas "we had to read ten books" and, as a result, acquired a deeper knowledge. "Even today I probably know things that maybe I shouldn't," she says.

Olayemi was under a great deal of pressure at the firm, but she was not afraid of being "thrown to the lions" and was stronger for the experience. Her best boss was Konyinsola Ajayi, the managing partner: "I admired his writing, his penmanship," she explains. After she left the firm and found that not everyone wrote like him, she realised how much she had learned.

After OALP she joined Sahara Energy Group, where she learned some important lessons about professional survival.

> *Within the scope of the law, they will do what it takes to get the job done. That's how it is. And sometimes now, when I'm saying something to my younger ones, and they're giving me excuses, I'm like, why are you giving excuses? Just get it done. Because that was the spirit I was taught – to just get it done.*

"Do what it takes to get the job done. That's how it is ... because that was the spirit I was taught – to just get it done."

Career progression

Olayemi enjoys talking about the lessons she learned from her first jobs. She doesn't really believe in luck; rather, she believes we must learn from what life gives us and make the most of those opportunities when we can.

Missing the private practice environment, in 2006, Olayemi left Sahara Energy Group after a year to join Templars, one of Nigeria's leading firms. She was hired to help managing partner, Oghogho Akpata, who led the energy practice. He felt that the firm needed a strong energy lawyer but Olayemi saw that Templars' finance practice needed strengthening and she believed that she would be able to have more impact in that sector because of her financial background.

The gender pay gap

Olayemi gives strong presentations and brought in business for the firm. She had joined Templars in 2006 as a partner, after just three years in law practice. She was then the only female partner in the firm, and also the youngest, and one of the things she liked about the managing partner was that he ensured her compensation was fair – when it came to remuneration, it simply wasn't relevant that she was a woman.

Olayemi says that in Africa, women are not always paid appropriately for their position, and that there is still a tendency to treat women's work as some sort of hobby – something to get them out of the house. There is an attitude that "you don't really need the money, your husband can afford it". She finds these attitudes annoying:

> *If you put both a man and a woman on a transaction, even if the woman is a partner, people will automatically defer to the man. Like, why? I would never do that.*

Olayemi stresses that women shouldn't just talk about gender imbalance; they must do something about it, especially as it is reliance on the wider family support network in Nigeria that makes the life of a working mother possible.

Becoming a partner

Did becoming a partner represent a big change for Olayemi? Absolutely.

> *When you're working on your own, you only have to take responsibility for your own actions. But when you're a partner, you can't be like that because you are responsible for other people. And even though I could do a particular piece of work in thirty minutes, I would have to delegate it to other people and let them*

> *struggle for three or four hours – if we don't give people that opportunity, they will never learn. So for me, that was a big change. I was forced to come out of my shell. I was forced to work more with people, and I was forced to sometimes ignore the fact that working with them would actually delay me because at that point, you have to be focused on developing their skills.*

Starting one's own law firm means also becoming the managing partner, something that did not come easily to Olayemi:

> *I may be good at managing, but it's not my natural skill. I love analysing issues, working on transactions, writing articles. I enjoy that. But now I don't read as much as I would like to. So I look for ways to go back to the things that I really enjoy.*

One thing Olayemi particularly enjoys is working with young lawyers. She likes their enthusiasm and the fact that they are "a blank slate", willing to learn, and much easier to teach than their older counterparts. Management takes her away from that.

Being her own boss

Olayemi left Templars after several years because she felt she had peaked and was no longer growing professionally. She wanted to be exposed to different challenges and had become restless and bored. With no immediate plans, she took some time off and went back to university to take a finance course. It was at this point that Olayemi started working from home and, as the workload grew, she hired two lawyers who worked from her garage. It was the start of running her own firm.

When asked about the origins of the name 'Sefton Fross', Olayemi explains that the first thing most Nigerian lawyers do when they are called to the Bar is register a law firm. She had one registered which was dormant but says that it had "a not so impressive name". So after coming up with alternatives, in various combinations, but not settling on one she liked, Olayemi relied on her intuition. The perfect name finally came to her one morning at 4am and Sefton Fross was born.

Money isn't everything

Olayemi says that almost every time she has changed jobs she has lost money – that if she had stayed at Templars, she would probably be earning more than she is now – but leaving was still the right thing to do.

> *I always tell young lawyers about my experience. If making money is your goal, you will not take the right decisions. You need to look inside yourself to find out what you want to be. And let those things*

"I recognise that people are in business to take risks. And the best you can do for them is to help them identify what they want – and advise them on their best possible option."

be your goal – step away from the money and do a good job. Focus on building a brand, building a reputation. They are the important things, right? It is better to be richer when you're older. So I tell them to think less about the money and focus more on the things that last.

And what are her clients looking for?

I think a lot of my clients like me for one major thing. They tell me all the time that I'm very commercial. You know, lawyers worry. We're risk averse. I try not to be like that. I look at the issues, and I tell clients: "These are the risks, and this is how you can mitigate them." I recognise that people are in business to take risks. And the best you can do for them is to help them identify what they want – and advise them on their best possible option. It's about saying "If that's really what you want to do, these are the ways you can do it in the safest way possible".

Management focus, direction and support

Olayemi believes that all law firms, large, small or somewhere in between, should focus on the quality of their work. Big firms should not chase deals at any cost and small firms should not pretend to be what they are not.

First and foremost she believes that the purpose of management is to give direction:

> *I think organisations go through separate phases of growth. And you need to get people to understand your vision. If you work with people who haven't embraced your vision, and you just tell them get on with it, they're going to find that difficult. So, it's just like democracy: democracy needs to mature to a certain level before it works. So, whether you are building a business or building a country or building an economy, you need direction. And for me, right now it's about giving directions and being very, very upfront with that. Because I've found that if I don't hold a very tight rein, things just run away.*

As part of her role as a manager, Olayemi has had to deal with COVID-19. She says that in Nigeria, as elsewhere, young lawyers do not always have enough space to work from home during lockdown. However, in Nigeria lawyers also have to contend with the added problem of constant interruptions to the electricity and so, to ensure that staff are kept productive and happy, Olayemi's firm bought solar panels for its employees' houses.

This practical, focused approach sums up Olayemi and her work at Sefton Fross. The aim is, simply, to "just get it done".

Advice to a senior or managing partner

- Make sure everyone knows your vision.
- Make sure the firm stays within its capabilities.
- Pay fairly, but don't pay anyone more than they are worth.

Olayemi Anyanechi
Founder and managing partner, Sefton Fross
o.anyanechi@seftonfross.com

Olayemi Anyanechi is the founder and managing partner of Sefton Fross, a leading law firm in Nigeria. She has more than 24 years' experience in banking and finance, mergers, acquisitions, corporate reorganisations, energy and natural resources. She has advised on some of the largest and most significant commercial transactions in Nigeria and is renowned for her outstanding knowledge of corporate and commercial law practice and a remarkable track record of closing deals.

Olayemi graduated top of her class at the University of Ibadan and she completed a master's degree in law at Wolfson College, Cambridge. She also has an MPhil in finance from the School of Oriental and African Studies, London.

She is the author of several articles and is co-author of two chapters – "Farmout agreements" and "Public procurement in the upstream oil and gas industry" – in *The Encyclopaedia of Upstream Oil and Gas*, Second Edition, published by Globe Law and Business in 2019.

Olayemi is recognised as one of Nigeria's topmost lawyers in corporate, financial as well as the energy and natural resources sectors by *Legal 500*, *IFLR1000*, *Who's Who Legal* and *Chambers*. She was recently recognised by Business Day as an *Outstanding Woman in Business Law, Project Finance,* for the year 2020.

She is currently the thematic lead, financial services, for the National Assembly Business Environment Roundtables (NASSBER). Until recently, she was chairperson of the Mergers, Acquisitions and Corporate Reorganisation Committee of the Nigerian Bar Association Section on Business Law (NBA-SBL).

© Bill Knight

Edward Braham

Former senior partner, Freshfields Bruckhaus Deringer LLP

Edward Braham was elected as the senior partner of Freshfields Bruckhaus Deringer LLP for five years from 2016. Freshfields is one of the world's leading law firms; a major business with a history going back over 275 years. The firm is headquartered in the City of London with offices across the world. In January 2021, Edward was succeeded as senior partner by Georgia Dawson.

Early years

Edward read law at Oxford University and came out top in his postgraduate degree – the prestigious Bachelor of Civil Law. When he started his studies, he had thought he might become a barrister (or possibly not go into the law at all), but he was recruited by Freshfields after two interviews, one over drinks at the Randolph Hotel and a more formal one the following day. He cannot remember what was said on either occasion but when he left the formal interview and went to pick up his mail, he found an offer from the firm already in his pigeonhole. He visited one other firm, who showed him out of the door at 1pm without a sandwich, but when he visited Freshfields they gave him lunch and a tour by someone who was "good fun and interesting". He was set for life.

The first piece of work he remembers was advice for John Grieves, who was the firm's leading corporate lawyer and who later became the firm's senior partner. It was about the impact of UN South Africa sanctions on Consolidated Goldfields, one of the firm's major clients. Edward had always believed that public international law had more to do with history, politics and power than with law, but he worked hard at his memo, and sought advice on house style from David Graham, one of the associates with whom he shared a room. He gave it to John and heard nothing. After a week he asked if it had been any help and John said, "Oh yes, I sent it off to the client". When Edward went to ConsGold's AGM some years later, he was startled to find it in the briefing pack for the board. Clearly, he had passed some sort of test. His views meant something.

Edward had a spell at the firm's New York office and was trying to decide whether to work in tax or corporate law on his return to London. The partner there, Peter Jeffcote, made his mind up for him by asking whether he wanted to be in charge of the discussion or not. He chose corporate.

Becoming a partner

Edward did well as an associate and in 1995 he became a partner. The firm was getting bigger and he was in the first batch of partners who had to undergo an interview for the promotion. He did not find that too difficult because those interviewing him "fortunately hadn't really worked out where the stumps were". He was asked one question he remembers: "How do you think clients would react if they knew that most of the detailed legal research was done by articled clerks and young lawyers?" Were he asked that question today, he would talk about what the partner brings to the table.

> *It takes time to research stuff and work out the detail. But the law is incredibly logical. And if you really understand the core principles then, if something doesn't make sense to you, it's almost always*

"It's about trying to properly understand where people are coming from. So I think the better you understand the law, the more likely you are to be able to help people do things they want to do."

> *because someone hasn't quite understood it. Or hasn't explained it well. Every now and then there is an exception, but you can always explain very clearly that this is just one of those times. A partner should have the understanding and experience to ask the right questions and evaluate the implications of the answers and the research itself.*

As a young partner he had "a really fantastic run": seven years of good clients and good deals, including the Lloyds TSB merger, ICI's purchase of Unilever's speciality chemicals business and Kingfisher's two-stage acquisition of Castorama. He worked often with Anthony Salz, who also went on to be senior partner, and Gavin Darlington, who also headed the global corporate practice. In different ways, both gave Edward a lot of responsibility and freedom, while themselves providing strategic leadership and credibility with the board. "It was terrific experience and I learned a lot."

Despite Edward's many successes, he says he was "only as good as his last cock-up". He had joined the firm with a reputation as obviously bright, being top in the Bachelor of Civil Law, and he was always grateful to David Graham who had helped him with the ConsGold memo at the beginning of his career because success brings trust and more success. Malcolm Gladwell's book *Outliers: The Story of Success* makes the point that those who are successful get better opportunities, better training and therefore yet more success – a virtuous circle of which Edward was clearly a beneficiary.

When asked if he likes the law, or whether he regards it as something which gets in the way of achieving his clients' objectives, he says:

> *So, not always, but usually, my clients are trying to achieve something very sensible. Their first idea on how to implement that idea can often be some way adrift of where it ought to be. I'll spend quite a lot of time trying to understand what a client really wants to do, as opposed to what they might have just said. And I've always thought that you need to understand a regulator's purpose in writing a rule. Because depending on what that purpose is, you can be braver, or less brave, on what the wording says. You can go to them and say, "Look, I know you've written it down like this, but my understanding is that you are trying to achieve that. So what we want to do really is okay". This looks like trying to change the law, but actually it isn't. It's about trying to properly understand where people are coming from. So I think the better you understand the law, the more likely you are to be able to help people do things they want to do and should be able to do.*

Edward believes that a good lawyer should properly support their client when making a difficult decision. Too often, and especially when dealing with multi-jurisdictional issues, lawyers will collate and summarise information, with a tendency to see the law they know best as the most important. They tend not to go the extra step in using their and their firm's experience to help their client synthesise the analysis, balance conflicting requirements and objectives and optimise the outcome. He wants to combine his and the firm's experience with that of the in-house lawyers so that together they can do things that they are unable to do on their own.

The move to management

Why did he move to management? He says that he wanted to be in a position where he could at least propose the agenda:

> *From very early on, every nine months I have always had a really sleepless night where I go through all the different things I could be doing. I've always gone through this cycle of thinking about all the alternatives. It's all driven by my subconscious and usually, by morning, I've decided that what I am doing is the most interesting thing to do. So I've gone into this sort of continuous reengagement. But sometimes it's taken me three or four months to decide what I want to do. The management stuff started, I guess, when we were going through a disappointing period in London.*

Edward started in 2005 when he was elected to the board and became leader of the private equity team in the London corporate group. As he left for a sabbatical the following year, he went to Ted Burke, the firm's managing partner, and told him the market was changing. "We had extraordinarily highly leveraged buyers making competitive public bids for infrastructure companies – transport, energy, water, data centres and the rest. The people with the M&A skills didn't know the individuals running these companies or their assets, and those who did know them didn't have the high-end M&A skills needed." Edward saw this as an opportunity and when he came back from sabbatical, Ted told him that his next job was to lead the infrastructure group with Nick Bliss, who knew the infrastructure market intimately. Together, they brought together the relevant partners and gave the market the integrated offering it was looking for.

Does he have any insights about getting lawyers to do what you want? "No," he says with a smile. But he relents. He says you have to be very clear about who is going to do what, when.

> *And you need to put yourself in the shoes of the people you are dealing with, particularly in an international firm like Freshfields. There is a different approach in, say, a US office and the Japanese office. You start with a base knowledge, but you have to top it up by talking to people. When I cut that bit short, that's when I get into trouble.*

Senior roles

Edward took over leadership of the corporate practice in 2009 and became senior partner in 2016.

> *When I took over the corporate practice, I was asking myself OK, what have I done, which justifies letting me do it? And I thought that, looking at the firm's offices around the world, there are only five that I haven't done a deal out of and I have slept on the floor of least half of them. So I told myself, you know what, you have learned a little bit about the world in the course of that.*
>
> *I know all my Asia partners because I've been on the ground long enough, doing real work, to meet them. Do I know them well? Some, yes, but certainly not all. Do other people know their market better than I do? Absolutely. But I've got that base knowledge. And one of the advantages to doing something like infrastructure, because by definition you're taking a cut across industry, you're hitting every practice, and you're hitting nearly every office. So you meet a whole different group of people that way.*

"By the time I became senior partner I had worked with a large number of partners, knew their and the firm's business and knew all of our partners at least well enough to know who they were and what they did."

My core theme for the corporate practice was that it needed to be better integrated, both within the practice and with the firm as a whole, as so much that is really interesting is on the margin of a practice. So with that mindset I always took a huge interest in whatever was going on with our clients and would always connect people when I thought there might be an interesting discussion to have. So by the time I became senior partner I had worked with a large number of partners, knew their and the firm's business and knew all of our partners at least well enough to know who they were and what they did.

Does Edward spend time with the junior lawyers? He says not enough, although he enjoys it.

One thing I do is try and make it clear to them that I don't expect them to get it right every time. And unless they're clear what they're doing, they should come back and talk. Indeed, I definitely expect them to come back and talk an hour or two after I've asked them to do something, because they'll probably have questions. And I often tell a story about a situation where someone had done something unbelievably unhelpful, but they had come and talked to me the moment it happened, and we therefore managed to stop it going wrong. We all make mistakes, but the key is to fix things quickly!

> *I know it's a bit scary for a young lawyer doing things with me, but I encourage them not to worry. Because I think that was what John Grieves did with me. He worked out very quickly what sort of person I was, and he gave me the freedom to make mistakes. But every now and then he'd stop and redirect me. I've tried to be the same. I've always tried to encourage people to get out of their comfort zone a bit.*

Management philosophy

As a lawyer and a manager, Edward will focus his energies on the things he thinks will really make a difference. The rest can just get done "in an OK way, because nothing's going to turn on that".

> *People say I'm strategic. I don't know what that really means. But if it means I will spend longer thinking about what we should be doing before I start applying huge amounts of effort into doing something then yes, I think I probably am.*

Does he see management as providing direction or offering a service?

> *On management, everyone has a view and many of our partners are very good at it. But the number of people who are truly supportive, when leadership matters, is very few and you should really treasure those people. Do I think the servant/leader approach is fundamentally right? Yes, it has to be right. The success of the firm derives from the success of everyone in the firm. And therefore, in that sense, you're facilitating to allow people to perform at their peak. But there are times you need to be really very brave in defining a path, and when everyone says "can't do, mustn't do" you stick to your guns. You listen very carefully to what they're saying but stick to your guns. It's a bit like those M&A deals where the first thing someone says is, "Gosh, this isn't going to work". And you probably had the same thought numerous times along the path, but for whatever reason you kept going because it's the right thing to be doing, and the client wants to do it, and you get somewhere that people aren't expecting. And I think it's the same in some of the really difficult things we've done. There have been long periods where people thought either it was mad or just simply unachievable, but we got to somewhere really good.*

Edward thinks that most people who are successful in life are completely committed to what they are doing. The parting advice from Andreas Fabritius, his successful predecessor as head of corporate at Freshfields, was to not take the job too much to heart. Edward says that in all honesty he would not claim to have taken that advice, but it helped him because he remembered it at difficult moments "when life gets in the way".

Edward acknowledges the value of management training, but it is the things that help him understand people that are really important: "After all, you can always have someone who can do good cash-flow systems." Freshfields has a handful of people who have done MBAs, but their value has often been in gaining insight into the client's business rather than managing at the firm.

The United States

Freshfields has an important and growing presence in the US and has opened in Silicon Valley during lockdown. Are the Americans different?

Edward says the US firms are helped by their massive internal market, and the willingness of their clients to pay fees. The internal market is competitive but at the end of the day an asset deal in 50 states is "really not very complicated" whereas an asset deal in 50 countries (and here Edward's eyes light up) "is a proper deal".

> *They enforce stuff in different ways. They go to court, we use regulators, and that drives some of the differences. You get hugely capable people who are very close to their clients. But even the most international will instinctively do things in a very American way. But they're right, because actually, that's what their clients want. And*

"People say I'm strategic. I don't know what that really means. But if it means I will spend longer thinking about what we should be doing before I start applying huge amounts of effort into doing something then yes, I think I probably am."

> *that is where I think we get it wrong. We say, "you're being American over here" but what we actually need to do is learn how to face off with an American client the way an American client truly wants and there are very few people indeed in the market who can do that.*

The bigger picture

Edward believes that Freshfields needs to be an open, sustainable business which over time makes a net contribution to society. The firm's five-year responsible business strategy brings together ethics and integrity and culture and diversity, as well as environmental impact, community investment and *pro bono*. He says he needed to lead from the top on this:

> *This is a much broader point. Ultimately our firm needs to be reflective of the society we serve. And if you look at our clients, they are often more diverse than we are. And they expect their legal advisers to be as diverse as they are. You can complain all you like, but at the end of the day, if it's a mismatch, it's going to come back to bite you.*
>
> *So there's a defensive reason for wanting to [be diverse] and the positive reason is well illustrated by the Freshfields Stephen Lawrence programme, a very successful scheme that not only focuses on black men from less socially mobile backgrounds, but from the start also deliberately targeted universities where we weren't so good at recruiting people. We found some truly fantastic talents.*
>
> *Are we recruiting the people the firm is going to need? If you're not doing a good job in achieving diversity, then it's highly unlikely you are, either because you're missing massive talent, or because you haven't got the mix of people the clients expect. And your decision making is going to be two dimensional, not more than that. Very good reasons to try to get this right.*

Like other senior partners, Edward believes that the firm does its best public policy work behind the scenes. It is not helpful to the firm to express views publicly that run counter to the culture of the place where the firm is doing business.

Key lessons

Edward has been walking the high wire ever since coming top in the Bachelor of Civil Law. What has he learned?

> *First, leadership. You won't get very much help on that. And ultimately, that's what matters most. Anyone who does help you on that is very special.*

And then the question of plans and reality. You've probably got a plan but there's more to this job than you'd ever thought of – not all of it productive. Events have a nasty habit of getting in the way. So with a combination of Brexit and pandemic we still managed to deliver [opening in] Silicon Valley. How? Well, the answer is because the goal was always clear, we kept moving towards it and when we developed the opportunity, we were able to capture it. So even when everything else is going wrong, keep your eye on those big goals and keep trying to move towards them.

And then the third piece of advice is just do your best. You will be worrying and if you're not, you probably should be. Whatever you do, there will always be someone who criticises what you've just done. You can draw strength from what goes well. And you can learn from the things that don't go as you want. Ultimately, you can only do your best.

Advice to a senior or managing partner

- Accept and fulfil the leadership role.
- Keep your eye on the big goals.
- Do your best.

Edward Braham
Former senior partner, Freshfields Bruckhaus Deringer LLP
edward.braham@freshfields.com

Edward Braham served as senior partner (executive chair) of Freshfields from 1 January 2016 to 31 December 2020. Previously he led their global corporate group and was a member of their executive committee for nearly six years. He also led their infrastructure and transport practice for three years and served on their elected board for five years.

He is recognised as one of the UK's leading M&A lawyers, acting for public companies, financial sponsors and financial institutions. Landmark transactions include: ICI's complex multi-jurisdictional purchase of Unilever's speciality chemicals division; the formation of dual-headed media company Reed Elsevier; Kingfisher's two-stage acquisition of Castorama; the take-private of retailer Debenhams, which changed the way takeovers are done in the UK; CVC's acquisition of Formula One; and acting for Anheuser Busch on its bid for Harbin Brewery, the first competitive public bid in China.

© Bill Knight

Melissa Butler

London office executive partner, White & Case LLP*

Melissa Butler is the London office executive partner of White & Case LLP, a firm recognised worldwide for its legal innovation and outstanding service to clients. The London office alone employs more than 400 lawyers.

Early years

Melissa is an American. She was educated at the University of Colorado and then studied for her law degree at Georgetown University in Washington DC. She says that she became a lawyer because she was convinced that she was going to "save the world and become an environmental lawyer". But as the American educational system "has a tendency to put you in quite a lot of debt", she had to find more lucrative employment. So she took a job as a corporate lawyer with a firm in New York – Thacher, Proffitt & Wood.

Melissa's scheduled start date with Thacher Proffitt & Wood was 12 September 2001, but she had pushed it back to 1 October, which proved to be an important decision as the firm's offices were in the World Trade Center. On 9/11, Melissa was in Kathmandu where she watched the terrorist attack on the Twin Towers on television "like it was a movie". It was hard to get information. Melissa had already worked in the firm as a summer associate and knew some of the people, so she was very concerned. Happily, everyone at the firm survived and made it out of the building. Melissa says that lawyers tend to have late start times and a lot of them hadn't yet reached the office when the planes struck.

By the time Melissa returned, the firm had found temporary offices in Midtown. The firm's principal client was Lehman Brothers and Melissa worked very hard in the financial and capital markets business. So hard, in fact, that she thought of quitting.

> *New York – really long hours. Not much of a social life. You find that you're just constantly cancelling plans and letting friends down and, you know, it's tough. I had actually thought about quitting. And I spoke to a friend who said, "You know, you are really good at this". She was actually a senior lawyer in my team, and she said, "You're really good at what you do. And so maybe instead of quitting, just try something different".*

Melissa had always wanted to live in Europe, so she was looking for a position there when she got a call from a recruiter who said they were seeking people to come to the White & Case London office to do public securities work. The interview went well, and she arrived in London on 27 August 2006, driving into London from Heathrow through the Notting Hill Carnival – the first time she had seen anything like that.

London calling

Her introduction to White & Case London was not in the office but at the Lancashire country house of one of the senior London partners, Francis Fitzherbert-Brockholes. The team stayed at a local hotel and

"Someone told me that you're not going to actually feel like a partner until there's incoming classes of people who've only ever known you in that role. I think there's a lot of truth in that, because especially in the beginning, people don't know the difference."

was invited to the house for a barbecue and "some clay pigeon shooting and other kinds of country pursuits that some people in England love to do". Melissa says that as a New Yorker "fresh off the boat" she found the whole thing "quite interesting".

> *It was actually quite an awkward way to meet because you were just kind of thrown in a lot of time. I remember sneaking out behind the back of the house and calling one of my girlfriends back in New York and puffing on a cigarette, and I go "My God, what have I done?" It was very awkward, but everyone was so wonderful and gracious and nice. And it was clearly very different from how things were done in New York.*

Melissa's first deal was for a Nigerian institution, Guaranty Trust Bank. This was the first Nigerian bank to access the international capital markets. Harvard case studies have been written about the bank's ability to maintain integrity in a corrupt environment. Before this assignment, the most interesting place Melissa had gone for due diligence was Ohio. Now she found herself getting vaccinations and taking a plane to Lagos. After that, her practice was largely built on doing deals in Africa – she is currently advising the Republic of Zambia on its debt restructuring.

Melissa likes the law:

Capital markets lawyers write prospectuses rather than actually go into court and do the kind of stuff you typically think lawyers do. But I do like the law. I like that you can give answers to things. I had a conversation with someone the other day. They were trying to do something. And I said, "What you want to do seems eminently reasonable to me as a normal person who kind of understands this stuff. But that's not why you've asked me. You've asked me because I'm a lawyer, and I have to look at what the four corners of the law say, and it's up to you as to whether or not you want to take that advice". So it was helpful in the sense that it wasn't just an opinion. It's actually grounded in something. And I like that, because I feel like there's too much these days of people just giving opinions or giving views. But I like being able to point to what you're saying and why you're saying it.

Melissa loves to get the call on a new assignment. It's always a thrill.

That's a validation every single time. There's that little jolt of excitement. I love it. It's a great feeling that someone trusts you and wants you to assist them. But in terms of the rest of the work, I do love the capital market stuff. I love the disclosure aspect. I love getting to know a company or country where I do a lot of sovereign work. We just closed a deal for Uzbekistan. The first time the Republic came to market was January 2019. And a year prior to that, it was illegal to publish any data about the Republic of Uzbekistan. It was a closed country. And then to go from that to within a year publishing a 250-page document that said everything you need to know to invest in the country... I mean, it was just such a dramatic shift, right?

Achieving partnership

Melissa was promoted in 2012. It was the last year when, theoretically at least, lawyers in the firm did not know whether they were up for partnership – they were called down to a meeting room where the other partners were assembled, with champagne. In fact, they usually did have a pretty good idea in advance. These days, of course, they have to prepare a business case for promotion. On the critical day Melissa "had the flu and felt terrible".

Partnership took some getting used to.

Someone told me that you're not going to actually feel like a partner until there's incoming classes of people who've only ever known you in that role. I think there's a lot of truth in that, because especially in the beginning, people don't know the difference. You were an associate yesterday; I'm not going to bow down to you. And you're not suddenly any more amazing or less amazing than you were the day before. It's not until there is a new class of people who have only ever known you as a partner, that you actually start to feel it. You actually start to believe it, and you actually start to act like it. And I think that there's a reason for that, right? I think you have to go to these things with some humility. It's not as though you can walk into the room on your first day of being a partner and say, "OK, here it is everyone!" – I mean, you have to grow into the role. You don't suddenly become something else.

I thought, I'm suddenly going to get access to all this information and look behind the curtain. It's something I've learned over the years that it just doesn't work that way. Things don't happen as intentionally as people think. There's a lot of working things out as you go along, at every level, in the firm and in life. And it's kind of understanding that there's not some sort of grand plan, and here's how you fit into it. And here's what you do. There's a lot of adapting and thinking on your feet and, you know, figuring it out.

White & Case is a very large firm and attending her first global partners' meeting, Melissa felt "humbled by the machinery". But today she has managed to peek behind the curtain and has a lot more ability to influence the people she works with. Just having the platform to communicate from has been important, especially this past year.

The move to management

In 2018, Melissa became executive partner in charge of the London office. She succeeded Oliver Brettle, who had held the job for ten years. She was asked to take up the role by Hugh Verrier, the firm's senior partner.

Melissa brought her own style to the job.

I felt very much that I had to be myself. And I don't know if other people thought this way, or I just was worried that other people thought this way. But you do worry that when you're not tough, and, you know, "My way or the highway", that people won't respect you. That people will think you're soft, and that people will think, "Oh, I don't need to listen to you".

I have heard that a few times in my career that, "You're too nice. You need to be tougher" but I've never stopped being nice. I've always thought being nice is really important. I saw a quote from Mr Rogers, I'm sure you've heard of him – I don't know if he's just a uniquely American character. He has a quote, a quite famous quote, that there's three paths to success. Three ways to be successful in

"I thought, I'm suddenly going to get access to all this information and look behind the curtain. It's something I've learned over the years that it just doesn't work that way."

life. The first is to be kind. The second is to be kind. And the third is to be kind.

And I do think that style of leadership was really validated this year, when leaders needed to be compassionate and empathetic in a way that they have not been asked to be or needed to be for a very long time. I think that's been an interesting experience. And you do see that people respond to that kind of leadership. A different style might not have been so successful.

There are times when Melissa has had to put her foot down and give firm direction. She does not like to do that:

I find it very hard. I seek to avoid it as much as I can, trying to find compromise and consensus, but when I've had to do it, I do it. I'll be honest with you, having to do it actually makes me want to quit being a leader because I really struggle with that conflict internally.

Building a vision

The London office of White & Case has 115 partners, 400 lawyers and a total staff of 800. Melissa is trying to get everyone behind a consistent vision for the office.

One of the best parts about this is the process of actually engaging with each other and talking about it. I could just sit down and write out an essay and send it around and say, "Here's the vision". But then it would just get stuffed away in an email folder. It won't happen if you don't go through the process of engaging with people and having these conversations to help people articulate for themselves. What kind of firm do you want to be a part of? What kind of firm is going to help you be more successful? What kind of office is going to help you be more successful? How should we set our salaries? What should our office space look like? What kind of clients do we want to attract? What kind of strategies do we want? If people aren't engaged in those discussions themselves and articulating them themselves, then, you know, it's just not going to work.

And when you start talking about these things you start to look under the rock a little bit more. That's when people start to talk about the things that are hard. The feelings of where things are unfair, or concerns about other partner behaviour, concerns about incentives. And financial incentives and how they don't always incentivise the right things. There's a lot that comes out of it and I think people appreciate having an opportunity to be heard.

"We definitely have to fit into the larger firm strategy – the firm's strategy is our strategy. There's no question about that. And that would be the same across different offices, but each of us has our own challenges, and there's no one-size-fits-all approach."

White & Case, Melissa explains, is a global firm, with a global strategy:

> *We definitely have to fit into the larger firm strategy – the firm's strategy is our strategy. There's no question about that. And that would be the same across different offices, but each of us has our own challenges, and there's no one-size-fits-all approach to dealing with the issues that each individual office has – how we hire people, how we train people, who our clients are, what our competitive pressures are: that's different in every office. We communicate with each other, we learn from each other, we share information about initiatives and what people are doing and it actually works quite well. In the sense that you feel like you are part of something bigger, and that's what your goals are, but you also feel very much that you have your own ability to do things the way you want.*

Working at White & Case

What does Melissa tell a new lawyer when he or she joins the firm?

> *Well, aside from the usual in terms of working hard and billing hours, we expect them to take hold of opportunities. We're a global firm – we have lots of things on offer. We expect people not to wait to be asked to do things, but to look for chances and opportunities to build their own careers. And we have strong expectations that we want people to take control of their own path. Some new joiners will become partners, and some of them won't. I think the most important thing for us is that, however long you're here at the firm, you get something out of that experience. Something positive, so that that you will look back fondly on your time and that you felt like it developed you as a lawyer and helped your career, wherever you end up.*

Diversity is very important, and Melissa takes it seriously:

> *We always strive to improve. It's definitely a journey and we constantly need to check ourselves. And it's not just hiring. Diversity is very broad term. We want to be a place that promotes not just diversity from an ethnic perspective, but also diversity of thought. So social mobility, different backgrounds, everything. You need a culture that promotes all of that – but it's not just hiring. This year has shown us that more than ever, with the experience of Black Lives Matter and the issues that have come to the surface around that. It's really about creating a culture where people feel that they belong. You can hire all the diverse people you want. But if they get here, and they feel like they don't belong here, because our culture says that we don't want people that look like you or think like you – then while your statistics may say you are diverse, you really aren't. That's the hard work.*

How does Melissa deal with that?

> *I start by verbalising it and saying that this is what we want you to do. And this is where you're safe. I spend a lot of time talking to other partners about this. We've spent some time, particularly this year, asking our Black employees to share their experiences of prejudice. We asked our them to share written stories of something that they've experienced. And then a couple of firm leaders, myself included, read out the stories to a meeting so they were not identified. It was a challenging experience.*

Melissa says that the job for women is still rather different:

> *I would be surprised if any of my male partners are sitting there in a meeting, doing the Ocado order on the phone under their desk, because they're going to run out of nappies. Which is something I have done multiple times in my career.*
>
> *I think where I have the most job satisfaction is when I feel like I'm part of a team. Stereotypically, some men seem to get job satisfaction when they feel like they're winning. Whereas in my experience, women tend to get job satisfaction when they feel like they are collaborating and working well with each other to achieve something.*

Lawyers and society

There is no doubt that in the US senior lawyers play a larger part in business and public life than they do in the UK. Melissa says that the changing nature of the practice of law may lead to changes in lawyers' role in society:

> *I think it would be great if lawyers were more engaged. I think there's a view that you don't go to lawyers for solutions, but just when you have a problem. I do think that the nature of practice is changing. Clients are not paying the rates law firms are charging for you to open a textbook and tell them what it says. They're paying for you to actually come up with solutions. They're paying you to innovate. They're paying you to help them improve their businesses. It's no longer a case where clients go off and do a deal and then come to lawyers and say, "draft the documents". I know that still does happen, but if you're going to do that, if you're that kind of lawyer, you're going to get commoditised pretty quickly. And you're going to find yourself with pretty limited options. I think that lawyers now really have to bring value to their clients in a way that they didn't have to do before. They have to bring industry knowledge. They have to bring market knowledge. You have to bring all that stuff, in addition to bringing your legal skill set. And*

that's how lawyers are going to stay in business. And I think that's something that the American firms have started doing very well.

Advice to a senior or managing partner

- Share your platform with others to promote other voices.
- Lead with kindness – do the right thing by people at the right time.
- Be authentic and – for women leaders – don't feel you need to copy traditional male leadership styles.

Melissa Butler
London office executive partner, White & Case LLP
mbutler@whitecase.com

Melissa Butler is the London office executive partner of White & Case LLP and also a partner in the firm's Capital Markets group. As such, Melissa is one of a small number of women law firm senior leaders in Europe.

In her practice role, Melissa has experience representing public and private issuers and underwriters in both equity and debt offerings in the United States pursuant to Rule 144A, and outside of the United States pursuant to Regulation S and SEC-registered offerings. Adept at navigating the legal intricacies of complex, cross-border transactions, she has advised on some of the most innovative and complex transactions in frontier markets in recent years. Her significant experience in handling major debt offerings in often volatile and challenging markets has made her a valued resource for sovereign clients. Her experience includes advising on the sovereign bond offerings by Angola, Ghana, Kenya, Montenegro, Nigeria, Rwanda, Serbia, the Ivory Coast and Uzbekistan, among others.

Melissa graduated from the University of Colorado with the highest distinction and holds a JD degree from Georgetown University Law Center.

** Any views expressed here are strictly those of the author and should not be attributed in any way to White & Case LLP.*

© Bill Knight

Michael Chissick

Managing partner, Fieldfisher LLP

Michael Chissick has been the managing partner of Fieldfisher LLP since 2013. Fieldfisher is a 25-office European firm headquartered in London with an annual turnover in the region of £250 million. The firm focuses on technology, financial services, natural resources and life sciences.

Early years

Michael read law at Leeds University in the 1980s because he felt he "wasn't able to do anything else", not being good at languages or science. He went to a state school and did not perform particularly well academically until he went on a visit to what would become his *alma mater*. After that, he started to work in earnest and got straight As at A level. At university he became fascinated by the way law underpins society. He did a summer school placement at Herbert Smith and stayed for articles. He says that nowadays getting a training contract is like "drawing the Willy Wonka golden ticket", but back then "it was all pretty simple". He didn't stay at the firm after qualification: "It was the Thatcher era and the firm was involved in a string of privatisations. I would have been a small cog in a big wheel."

Margaret Thatcher had another influence on Michael's career. In 1988, section 28 of the Local Government Act banned the 'promotion' of homosexuality in Britain's schools. As a gay man, Michael did not feel comfortable with the atmosphere in the United Kingdom and went to Amsterdam to join a law firm with an English practice. He worked in a Dutch canal house for 18 months. He describes it as "wonderfully genteel. Everyone spoke perfect English". But there were no prospects and in 1991 he returned to London to work for Hopkins & Wood, which subsequently merged with Hobson Audley. It was there that he realised that his future lay in computer law – long before it was called tech or IT. He worked on Acorn's joint venture with Apple to establish Advanced RISC Machines, now known as ARM. He was at "a really cutting-edge law firm that was doing incredible work".

Michael always liked the business of the law:

> *I'm not the type of lawyer that gets excited about a new case coming out or anything like that. It's more the mechanics and the business of the law which attracts me. I'm not a huge risk-taker. I like the security. But the big highlight was bringing in the client, doing the work, billing the client and seeing the money coming in. That was the bit that excited me more than developments in the law.*

While at Hopkins & Wood Michael read for an LLM at London University, specialising in telecoms, IT and competition law in order to give him the academic foundation he needed. He did this part-time and was "pretty busy". Then after spells at Hammond Suddards and the US firm Coudert Brothers, he joined Field Fisher Waterhouse in 1996 at the age of 30 as a salaried partner.

Fieldfisher

At the interview for his partnership at Fieldfisher, Michael "told them a story". He was acting for Colt Communications at the time and they had come to him to negotiate wayleaves for their cables.

> *They had been sending out these 10-page agreements to be negotiated and I came up with a new agreement and made it into a form with all the legals on it. I worked with an external designer to get it right. So, I had a client who had been spending huge numbers of hours negotiating deeds and once I redesigned it, they did it as a standard form. They loved it. Nobody challenged it. It was just psychology.*

Michael inherited the Fieldfisher technology practice from Anthony Landes, who was leaving the firm to join Andersen Consulting. Landes went out of his way to introduce his clients to Michael, who counts this as an important piece of good fortune and an example of how a lawyer should behave.

> *I thought "we can grow this" and that was where I made my mark – in going for growth. I'm not a genius lawyer. I'm not the world's best academic lawyer. But I had an idea which was that this is a good area of law and we can grow it. We were very successful in doing so over the next few years.*

"The big highlight was bringing in the client, doing the work, billing the client and seeing the money coming in. That that was the bit that excited me more than developments in the law."

Partnership was different.

> *I had never been a partner before, I didn't really understand partnership, I had never really been a leader before. I had started a couple of years previously thinking about clients and business development and winning work. That was the real challenge, and then recruiting someone and then you have the responsibility of feeding someone.*

Michael moved up rapidly from salaried partner.

> *I've always believed that in a law firm your status, credibility and remuneration all depend on fees and I was in the right place at the right time. I was also able to rebadge myself several times. It was always commercial law. I stopped doing corporate law. And we started off saying we were doing multimedia law and then we became internet law specialists and then it was e-commerce law. And then it became digital law then it became outsourcing. It was always the same, but I was quite good at rebadging.*

> *Building a team was the bit I enjoyed. I joined in 1996 as the only partner and over the next 15 years, growing it to a £10 million practice with 12 to 15 partners. Award-winning – all of that stuff. I don't actually rate the directories and the awards but that whole thing – the recognition – that was good.*

The move to management

Michael describes his move to management as "a bit complicated":

> *Traditionally, leadership had been done by pre-retiring partners. Most of them did three years and retired, some didn't even like it and were dragged into the role. I had always had this radar for opportunities. So I knew someone in Allison & Humphries, which was a boutique firm doing work for the BBC and I engineered a merger in 1998. I just had a good instinct. So many lawyers just look at their own practice. I was always looking for opportunities. And one of the partners at Allison & Humphries who I got to know became managing partner – Moira Gilmore. And she was our managing partner for a while, so although I wasn't on the board, I knew the managing partner well. Unfortunately, she got cancer and passed away.*

> *And then there was a bit of a leadership vacuum in the firm, and effectively I became a sort of interim managing partner when there was no one around to do it.*

Michael's 'and then' is something of an elision. It covers a period of turbulence in the firm from 2007 to 2012, with partners at loggerheads and two failed merger discussions with Lawrence Graham and Osborne Clarke. However, by 2013 things had settled down and Michael was left to reinvent the firm.

> *Time and time again, the people who do rise to managing partner have had good practices. I had built one of the most successful practices in the firm. And I always tried to learn from the tech companies I worked for. I tried to introduce new things, not revolutionary but say, mentoring, that I'd seen in the clients. I was working in a new way.*
>
> *So I did it on an interim basis for 10 months when there was a vacuum. And then things turned around quite quickly. It didn't actually take that much. I'm not going to say I'm a managing genius. But my predecessors hadn't really energised the firm and done some of the people stuff. It isn't complicated. It's often common sense but often overlooked.*

Michael discovered that the business service people in the firm were "pretty unloved" and nobody was really talking to them. He sat down with them and started to involve them in the management of the firm and to recognise their importance.

Bold steps

Then Michael took some significant decisions.

> *I suppose the reason I'm still here eight or nine years later as managing partner was that I moved us six years ago to the new building. We were in three buildings in what then was a very unexciting part of the City – the Minories. We'd moved there in 1989. The buildings were well past their sell-by date. Everyone had big offices and round tables, but we were also quite fractious because we had two main buildings and people would say, "That building wouldn't like it". We weren't in great shape. We were limping along. In those days, we still had a European legal alliance. We were friends with a few firms, but not an integrated European law firm. We could see Bird & Bird and Simmons & Simmons going much faster on the European stuff.*
>
> *I think the main things I did were to grow the European operations and move the firm. We had to pay a multi-million-pound break fee on the property. We didn't have to leave, but we had a break option which had only been put in because it was so expensive. I just thought we've got to do something; we can't stand still. I pioneered the idea to move from 135,000 square feet to 82,000 square feet. Let's rebrand the firm Fieldfisher, let's move to open plan. Not that*

"Time and time again, the people who do rise to managing partner have had good practices. I had built one of the most successful practices in the firm. And I always tried to learn from the tech companies I worked for. I tried to introduce new things, not revolutionary but say, mentoring, that I'd seen in the clients. I was working in a new way."

radical now as I sit here, but seven years ago, it was still quite radical for a traditional law firm to go open plan. And really difficult to get through the firm. Many people voted against the move. The fit-out was expensive. People just didn't want to move into open plan. They thought it was the end of the world. Partners sent me academic studies saying our productivity would crash. But in the end, only one person left on the back of the move.

So my flagship thing was, in one go, moving to new offices, new website, new brand. Leaving all the old paper behind. Changing overnight the systems and the way we worked. And it worked; it could have gone wrong and there were very hairy moments. We got rid of the phones on the desk. I brought in a lot of technology and notwithstanding the doomsayers, it did work. It repositioned the firm. I think, for me, it could be a Harvard case study. Because we were a slightly tired mid-tier legal firm with not a great reputation in the legal media. And overnight we moved to one of the best buildings in London. And it transformed the firm. I know transformation is a word that is bandied around by lots of management consultants, but we actually did it – in terms of internal perception, client perception and media perception.

Using technology

By focusing on technology, Michael hitched a ride on a rocket ship.

"I say time and time again to our young lawyers, give the advice, then pick up the phone to the client. Say hi. How are you? How was the advice? Are there any questions? Is there anything I can do?"

The firm has a successful office in Silicon Valley doing UK law and by moving offices and having a smaller footprint, the firm had money to invest in technology. Michael says that the young lawyers were more interested in the quality of their laptop, headset and wi-fi than in having a big office:

> *I wanted people to collaborate, I wanted to get people talking. It was all about people and business. So I built lots and lots of breakout spaces, coffee shops, cappuccino bars, places for people to huddle – all wi-fi enabled. And a few things didn't quite work the way we planned. But by and large, until COVID came along we had an open collaborative workspace. I wanted to stop people sending an email to someone who was 10 metres away. I was getting people talking. That's still my thing and something I'm still pushing. It's all about the people. I say time and time again to our young lawyers, give the advice, then pick up the phone to the client. Say hi. How are you? How was the advice? Are there any questions? Is there anything I can do? And it's a real struggle, because all they want to do is email and IM. So I have this office which is open and collaborative, full of people having coffee. And you know, actually, we've doubled our turnover since I became managing partner.*

Michael says he was inspired by his tech clients: "Very entrepreneurial, very can do. Willing to fail, take some big risks. All that stuff was relevant to me."

Managing a law firm

Fieldfisher has an executive board, chosen by Michael, which includes the heads of finance, business development and IT. Michael insists that each board member acts in the interests of the firm as a whole, rather than in the interests of his or her department. The senior partner chairs a supervisory board and continues to do client work.

Michael does not believe that corporate executives can run a law firm successfully:

> *You bring someone in from British Airways or Marks & Spencer and they immediately come in and start saying OK, close that office, sack him/her, etc. And then it feels like nothing's happened. The office is still there, no one's been sacked and what's going on? Law firms should be more business orientated, but each one's got its own unique culture, and people come in and they can't work out where the power is. There's full equity, fixed equity, the international partners – you need to understand how to get things done in an organisation where the organisation structure diagram gives you no clue.*

Although Fieldfisher has offices in Silicon Valley and China, it is still basically a European firm. Michael has resisted pivoting fully to Asia or America.

> *We happen to have an office in Silicon Valley, but we don't do US law. It's about English lawyers providing fast on-the-ground support to tech businesses. And I like that model. In Europe, we're all within two hours' flying time from each other. I think there's a real cohesion when we can meet. You know, if everyone's two hours away, then you can have lots and lots of better meetings, managing partner meetings, service line meetings; we can get together. And no one's turning up with jet lag because they travelled 12 hours. So there's a big focus for us on face-to-face meeting. Before COVID it was all about getting together, meeting each other, seeing each other, having some fun together as well.*

Do the foreign offices make money?

> *Yes, they do. It's always difficult because London's the European and global centre. Financially, opening new offices is an area where managing partners get over-excited. I've kept us focused. I've had loads of opportunities to do stuff in the Middle East and avoided them all. Everyone I know who's gone out there has lost a small*

fortune in Dubai, Doha, Saudi, Emirates, etc. I come at it from a business point of view. I don't see international as vanity projects. So actually, they all stand on their own two feet very well.

I really care about the staff. I care about the clients. But I've always seen my ultimate shareholders as the partners. I'm here to try and make sure they're successful. Because if we are successful, then people want to join us. People won't leave, and that's good for the staff. I admire many of the London law firms who have stuck to their knitting and remained UK-centric. Many managing partners get excited about offices in exotic locations and often those collaborations do not make real strategic sense, such as the rush a few years ago for UK-headquartered firms to merge with Australian firms.

Social responsibility

Michael is very positive about corporate social responsibility:

I've seen a huge change in my time in the profession. Social awareness has grown immensely. I think there's a lot going on that isn't reported. We've got people helping with reading and writing in schools in Tower Hamlets. I think that's changed a lot. And I'm not

"I really care about the staff. I care about the clients. But I've always seen my ultimate shareholders as the partners. I'm here to try and make sure they're successful. Because if we are successful, then people want to join us. People won't leave, and that's good for the staff."

going to knock the profession. You know, I see huge changes – people from different backgrounds and lots of efforts made to be as inclusive as possible. So I think it's lots of ticks for the profession. We could do more, of course, but the changes have been immense. And all for the better. And I think it's in the DNA – in the heart. I see people who are genuinely committed whereas 20 years ago, it was all a bit lip service. I think it's changed the people in it, too, because it's the right thing that they want to do. They genuinely want to work in a diverse workplace. I'm pretty positive about what the profession is doing and, speaking for my firm, I think it's done not to tick boxes, not to make clients happy. Not that we're shouting about it – we do our bit – but it's done for the right reasons.

Advice to a senior or managing partner

Michael thinks that the role of the managing partner is to lead and let the business professionals do the managing. He believes that the key service managers in IT, business development and finance should sit at the top table.

- Make partners feel that they are running the firm. Then you get 200 stakeholders who genuinely feel involved.
- Get the right team around you – good friends who can tell you not to do things, and good business professionals who are motivated to look after you.
- Don't get bogged down in the details – don't write thirty pages of strategy; you add value by having a vision and bringing people along.

Michael Chissick
Managing partner, Fieldfisher LLP
michael.chissick@fieldfisher.com

Michael Chissick is managing partner at Fieldfisher, based in the London office. He joined the firm in 1996 as a partner having trained at a Magic Circle firm and was a technology lawyer before becoming managing partner in 2012. He has a first-class law degree as well as a master's in law from the University of London.

He is committed to leading and growing the firm in a fast-changing economic and regulatory environment. He has led the firm through a major transformation and change programme to ensure it remains ahead of the pack by introducing advanced technology and new products, growing its European footprint and ensuring the firm provides the best in client service.

A key focus is ensuring the firm plays a key role in the community and undertakes extensive corporate social responsibility activities and *pro bono* work. He is also committed to ensuring the firm is a diverse place to work.

© Pablo Tribello https://pablotribello.com

Rafael Fontana

Senior partner, Cuatrecasas

Rafael (Rafa) Fontana is the senior partner of Cuatrecasas, one of the leading Spanish law firms, with offices across Spain, Portugal and Latin America as well as global cities such as Beijing, New York and London. When Rafa joined the firm in 1983, the total complement of staff was 19; today, the firm has over 1,700 employees. Rafa built the firm with Emilio Cuatrecasas, his lifelong friend.

Early years

Rafa read law at the *Universitat Autònoma de Barcelona*, graduating in 1977. He discovered that he had a penchant for tax law, which at the time was not considered "real" law in Spain; rather, it was seen as an administrative matter for accountants. There were no requirements for professional qualifications in those days so after five years of study Rafa opened an office in Barcelona, in partnership with another lawyer who had a practice outside Barcelona. His first client was a dentist, for whom he filed a personal tax return, charging him 5,000 pesetas (about €30).

Rafa's brother had worked for Arthur Andersen, the accountancy firm, and told him that they were looking for a tax lawyer in Barcelona. He encouraged Rafa to apply and he got the job. At the time it was forbidden for accountants to advise their audit clients, so Rafa was free to give tax advice to the clients of the other audit firms. He had a very happy time at Arthur Andersen, learning to work in teams, developing a common approach and learning a common professional language to enable people in the international firm to work together. He was sent to the Andersen Center for Professional Education in St Charles, Illinois, known informally as "Andersen University". Nothing like it existed in Spain and Rafa was astonished. He also learned about professional ethics. Today, the name of Arthur Andersen has been sullied by its collapse, but it was a fine firm when Rafa was there. He is still in touch with good friends he made there.

In 1983 Rafa received an offer he could not refuse from Emilio Cuatrecasas, the grandson of the founder of the Cuatrecasas law firm, whom Rafa had known at school. Cuatrecasas was a tiny firm specialising in tax with a total headcount of 19, including the senior partner's driver. Emilio had the vision to see the benefits of combining Rafa's international firm experience with a local firm and offered to double his salary.

Expanding the firm

The senior partner of the firm in 1983 was Pedro Cuatrecasas, Emilio's father. Emilio told his father that he would stay with the firm if he became managing partner, otherwise he would go. The older partners agreed, but "on condition that you don't affect the profits". Rafa was appointed as a partner and Emilio told him that over the next two years, they would work together to increase the firm's turnover from 100 million pesetas to a billion pesetas. Rafa saw it as his role to keep Emilio's feet on the ground.

When Rafa joined the firm it had offices in Barcelona and in Bilbao; the latter had been opened by Emilio's grandfather when he escaped to the Basque country from the civil war in Barcelona in 1936. When

"I cannot conceive of being a good lawyer without being a good person. I will say that one of the key characteristics of Cuatrecasas is being very proud of being a member of it."

Franco imposed a national tax regime on the Basque country after the civil war, the firm was well placed to advise on tax in Bilbao, but Cuatrecasas had no office in the capital, Madrid.

Rafa started the Madrid office in 1987 with two colleagues who had worked with him at Arthur Andersen. Rafa and Emilio shared a bedroom in the office. They had two challenges: to change the firm from a tax specialist to a full-service commercial firm; and to conquer Madrid. At the time there were two market-leading firms in Spain, both headquartered in Madrid: J&A Garrigues and Uría Menéndez. Emilio and Rafa opened in the same street as Garrigues and set out to add Cuatrecasas to the list. How did they do it?

> *The secret is trying to hire people better than you. We have a golden rule. In order to join the firm, you have to speak English very well, better than my bloody English, which is terrible. You have to have a doctorate, interesting experience, and so on. That's what we call the golden rule. So 10 years ago, 15 years ago, I wouldn't have been able to join the firm. I wouldn't have fulfilled those requirements.*

Cuatrecasas could not only rely on organic growth; they had to make lateral hires, otherwise it would not have been possible to expand the firm into new areas. They always hired locally.

Emilio spoke no English at that time and in 1987 he decided to spend six months in London learning the language, studying and finding out about the operations of the City's large firms. He left Rafa in charge of the firm's day-to-day management. Emilio's talent was to look to the future. He was very good with expansion – but "not so good with prices". Emilio and Rafa interviewed every lateral hire.

Rafa and Emilio were close friends, partners in the firm and partners outside the firm in real-estate investments. Until the firm got too large, all the equity partners participated in some real-estate deals, buying the offices in which the firm worked and leasing them back to the firm at market value. As the business grew, transactions such as these became impossible.

Cuatrecasas has expanded across Spain and Portugal and is strong in Latin America because of the language and the civil law base. The firm has 29 offices in 14 countries including Mexico, Colombia, Chile and Peru – always hiring locally. In Europe, the firm has relationships with Chiomenti, Gide Loyrette Nouel and Gleiss Lutz. Cuatrecasas has to compete with the global firms, but they do well against them. Rafa believes that the Anglo-Saxon approach combines well with the Latin:

> *The cocktail is very good. The way you work, the rigour and so on and the way a Latin lawyer works, being closer to the client, trying to understand what the client wants and becoming a friend, and so on. That makes you makes a very attractive lawyer.*

Management insights

Rafa believes very strongly in the power of personal relationships and personal fulfilment:

> *I cannot conceive of being a good lawyer without being a good person. I will say that one of the key characteristics of Cuatrecasas is being very proud of being a member of it. When I speak to our people, I try to finish my speeches by telling them, "Always try to be happy". If you analyse successful people in history, you see from Mahatma Gandhi to Leonardo da Vinci to Bill Gates, they love what they do – they love it. They have a vocation and I try to ask our people to be the same. If you are here, it has to be because you love what you do. And if not, let's look for a solution. Let's look for another role in Cuatrecasas because there are plenty of places where you can work.*
>
> *And this takes up a lot of time. I need to communicate well and listen to people – not just the partners. Everybody knows that I love to sit down with young associates who have been in the firm for a few years and I find out things that I would never know from the partners.*

And I am very strict with the values of the firm, very firm with the ethics, and if there is somebody who doesn't follow them, I don't care if they are a very good rainmaker or whatever. I don't want them.

Rafa is proud of the firm's IT. More than 50 engineers are employed in the IT department across the business. When the pandemic struck, they were able to move to working from home quickly and efficiently. Every Monday at 9am, Rafa sends his partners, of counsels and business professionals a bulletin to say what he is doing and what is going on in the firm.

Using IT enables the offices to report to the firm's management in detail.

We empower our people. We create tiny groups, with a partner in charge and we choose somebody from the administrative department in order to help manage that group. So, for example, they each have an HR professional. They have their own accounts; they have their own P&L so you can you know if each group is making a profit or a loss. We empower each unit that we form. We empower London, we empower New York, we empower Shanghai. Everyone is empowered and reports to the managing partner.

The same principle applies in the larger offices, where each department has its own P&L. Equity partners share the profits of the whole firm. With a few exceptions, the ratio of earnings among the equity partners is 4:1. Points are decided by an elected committee. Partners can move up quickly, but they can move down only slowly. Assessment is made on the basis of fee-earning and profitability but also on intangible factors such as reputation, business development and the results of the 360-degree assessment to which each partner is subject.

The finances of the firm are transparent within the partnership. Rafa says that when he joined Cuatrecasas, it was a family business; now it is an institutional firm. Partners can easily see their performance and the performance of their group and their peers across the firm.

The firm has number of business professionals – IT, communications, HR, business development and a general manager who runs the offices day to day. They all report to the managing partner. The firm is run by a 12-partner board and the general manager is invited to attend meetings. One board member is responsible for the offices outside Spain and Portugal.

Rafa says that he tells the associates that lateral hires are not there to block their progression, but rather to expand the firm's practice:

"I need to communicate well and listen to people – not just the partners. Everybody knows that I love to sit down with young associates who have been in the firm for a few years and I find out things that I would never know from the partners."

> *Look, this guy or this lady is here to make the cake bigger. If they don't, they will leave. And that's what happens. Our experience is that when the organisation isn't gelling, then whoever joined the firm, leaves the firm.*

In the 1990s, the firm made many lateral hires. They make fewer now, but two years ago they recruited Spain's former deputy prime minister, Soraya Sáenz de Santamaría, described by the media as "the most powerful woman in Spain since the return of democracy". An expert in public administration who advises clients on corporate governance, she is a member of the firm's board. Rafa believes that hires like these shows that Cuatrecasas is a different kind of law firm.

Embracing diversity

Diversity is important for Cuatrecasas. A majority of the firm's associates are women but at partner level the number drops to 16%. Rafa believes that the firm should not be losing that amount of talent and part of its strategic plan is to make changes with a view to retaining more women. Soraya Sáenz de Santamaría is leading the changes. For example, all the boards who run the firm – including the committee which recommends associates for partner – will be composed equally of men and woman. At present, the firm has time limits for each stage of an associate's progression – up or out. But this is not flexible enough to accommodate periods of maternity leave and will change. Rafa says that when a woman runs an organisation, many more women get promoted to senior positions. In Rafa's view, changes like this are good for Cuatrecasas and good for society as a whole.

In 1991, the firm created the Cuatrecasas Foundation. Its flagship activities are the Manuel Olivencia Award for Good Corporate Governance and the creation of the Spanish *Pro Bono* Foundation (*Fundación Pro Bono España*), which brings together many members of the legal world to develop *pro bono* projects in Spain.

In 2014, after more than 20 years as managing partner of Cuatrecasas, Rafa stepped down to become president of the firm. He had to choose his successor as managing partner and he says that this decision was the most difficult of his career. There were a number of excellent candidates, but he remembers that one senior partner came to see him and told him to choose someone he absolutely trusted, which is what he did. He chose Jorge Badía.

Rafa plans to retire in two years or so, when he will be 69, but he still works, from time to time, with clients. He has become a corporate lawyer.

"Be somebody who wins the client's trust and helps them take decisions. I don't want the client to ask me about the consequences of a decision which they have already taken. No, please ask me before!"

What I ask my partners to do, which not everybody can do, is to be somebody who wins the client's trust and helps them take decisions. I don't want the client to ask me about the consequences of a decision which they have already taken. No, please ask me before! Right now I have very few clients but I have very good relations with the top clients of the firm wherever they are. That's what I do.

Rafa has a number of board appointments and his partner is an Olympic rider who has established an equine care foundation. He expects to keep busy in retirement.

Advice to a senior or managing partner

- Earn the trust of your partners.
- Hire people better than you.
- Be happy.

Rafael Fontana
Senior partner, Cuatrecasas
rafael.fontana@cuatrecasas.com

Rafael (Rafa) Fontana started his career at Arthur Andersen and in 1983 joined Cuatrecasas as a lawyer in the Tax Practice. He was made partner in 1985 and was the firm's managing partner for over 20 years. In 2014, he was made senior partner.

A tax expert, Rafa particularly focuses on family business group planning and mergers, acquisitions and joint ventures of national and international business groups.

He has led the Cuatrecasas international expansion process, including the opening of offices in Mexico City, Bogotá and Beijing; and the consolidation of a European alliance with leading firms in France (Gide), Italy (Chiomenti) and Germany (Gleiss Lutz).

Throughout Rafa's outstanding career, he has advised on and participated in the strategic planning of some of Spain's and Portugal's most significant transactions. In addition to managing the firm's business, he is an active player in Spain's business arena.

© Rob Clayton

James Palmer

Former chair and senior partner, Herbert Smith Freehills

James Palmer was chair and senior partner of Herbert Smith Freehills from 2015 to April 2021. HSF is a global law firm with 26 offices worldwide. Known for its dispute resolution and corporate work, the firm is one of the world's leading professional services businesses. James is based in the firm's London office.

Early years

James was brought up partly in Asia. He was educated at Winchester College and read law at Cambridge. He thought about reading economics, but his maths wasn't good enough. In the end he read law because he did not know what else to do and his father was a lawyer. James says that he didn't want to compete with his father so he thought he would go into business, but subsequently did join the profession with articles at Herbert Smith. He had a 2:2 in his second year and his offer from the firm was conditional on his getting a 2:1 in finals. James thought everyone's offer was subject to such a condition and it was only later that he discovered that the condition had been added especially for his offer.

James liked Herbert Smith on sight. While other firms wanted to talk about his background and education, Herbert Smith were more meritocratic and had an international flavour, which suited his upbringing. James could see women doing the interviewing and students from other races and backgrounds waiting to be interviewed. He thought it was the firm for him.

He was "bored stiff" by his preparation for the professional exams at the College of Law and stopped attending lectures. He got a formal letter warning him that the College might expel him. His father, normally a quiet man, was unhappy. He told James that he wouldn't have cared if James hadn't done the course but to sign up for something and not see it through was not right. Mortified, James started work again and just scraped through the professional exams. On his first day at Herbert Smith in 1986 he was late for work, because he was coming in from Venezuela and his flights were cancelled. He was briefed by Mrs Trew, "the only person in HR", and by Bernard Baringer, the librarian.

On qualification, he became a corporate lawyer. During articles he had spent time in Hong Kong where the firm acted for the Hong Kong Government in the bailout of the Futures Exchange in the crash of 1987. That meant James was given a lot of responsibility on other work. Fred Kinmonth, the partner in charge there, proposed that on return to London, James should join the corporate group under Edward Walker-Arnott. James considers himself to have been lucky to work for Walker-Arnott and Margaret Mountford, who were keenly interested in developing young lawyers. He went to his first hostile bid defence meeting, on his own, at eight-weeks qualified.

> *I made a Horlicks of it. I kept saying "I'll have to speak to Mr Walker-Arnott afterwards" – but you do learn.*

He spent time in the 1990s doing restructurings and private and public mergers and acquisitions which gave him exposure to senior partners in other firms, who thought highly of him.

> *You know what it's like, if you click with people elsewhere, they talk to the directories, because they don't know anyone else. And you do build a reputation. And I look back and, honestly, this is not some sort of gracious false modesty – I really passionately believe it – I was so lucky.*

The path to partnership

James became a partner in Herbert Smith in 1994 at the same time as his contemporary, David Paterson. They were not expecting to be made partner, but two other senior associates had turned down offers of partnership because they were pregnant and did not want to rush their decisions on balancing parenting and partnership, just before the beginning of the new partnership year.

> *Richard Bond, who was head of corporate, and Edward, who was by then senior partner, called David and me into his room together and he said, "Well, hello, David, hello, James, we've decided we're going to make you both partners. I haven't told the partners yet. I'm sending a memo out today. And they'll all be supportive, so don't worry, and congratulations". And then we got £2,000 pay rises, which we later discovered was less than everybody else who was made partner then.*

James says that Herbert Smith was a reasonably open firm and tended to treat senior associates like partners, so at first he didn't notice a great deal of difference in his status within the firm. But then he had to start to manage people:

> *And I was a pretty rubbish supervisor. I was nice and supportive and honest, and those kinds of things, but I didn't understand about letting go. We had two small children. We started having children when I was an associate, so we weren't as well paid at the time, and my wife stopped working. And, you know, when the second one was a few months old, it was pretty difficult because mostly I was just full-tilt busy. I was doing the electricity-generating companies privatisation – the biggest privatisation of the 90s – and I had absolutely amazing responsibility. The most interesting work you could have, but I was under so much pressure at work. And how stupid can you be when you look back, but I was just used to working, working, working.*
>
> *So I went and saw a friend of mine who was a partner at Russell Reynolds, the head-hunters. We'd been at university together. I said, "I need to do something different. I really like law but I just can't*

work as hard as I am at the moment". And our conversation when something like this:

> *"Tell me, James are you working for some quite difficult people?"*
>
> *"No, no, they're lovely. You know, they're really supportive. They're really nice."*
>
> *"So have you got some really ghastly clients, James, really making your life miserable?"*
>
> *"No, the clients are demanding, but they're really appreciative."*
>
> *"Are you not feeling great about some of your colleagues, do they really resent you?"*
>
> *"No, my colleagues are lovely."*

Anyway, after about an hour and a half of me whinging about how this job was unsustainable and impossible, he said to me, "James, I've got something for you". And I said, "Well, that's great. You know, in seven weeks' time, between two and three in the afternoon, I might have a half-hour window when I could do an interview".

And he said, "No, James, there's no interview for this job".

I thought to myself, well, I know I'm good!

And he said, "No, James, you stupid jerk. It's the job you've already got. You just need to take control of how you work".

And I got that advice when I'd been a partner a year. And it was honestly the best advice I've ever been given in my career.

So I was bad at managing people, bad at delegating. And I'm still not perfect at it. But I had absorbed an interest in developing other people. I was interested in being liked, and in being nice to people. And so I think I started to become a lot better.

James has enjoyed an exciting career. One deal that stands out for him was the defence of the 1989 Hoylake bid for BAT where James Goldsmith put together a consortium to take over British American Tobacco for $22 billion – a huge bid at the time. The privatisation of the electricity-generating companies was also memorable because it went wrong. James was acting for the underwriters and the electricity regulator launched a pricing enquiry, which caused a steep fall in the share price. Slaughter and May were acting for the government and

"You do your best. You learn from things, you beat yourself up about the odd thing, but you have to be willing to fail. You pitch for a client and you don't win. Well, if you can't cope with that you can't be successful."

behaved to the young James Palmer "like complete gents". The experience launched James as someone who knew something about investment banks, because "it wasn't just doing the deal, it was understanding the regulation and the policy behind it". James also remembers the Freeserve IPO, which brought a large amount of dotcom business in its wake.

The move to management

In 1997 James "carried the bag" for Richard Fleck, a senior Herbert Smith partner who played an important part in the firm's international relations. James went with him to meet senior people from law firms in Europe and the United States and as a result became interested in law firm strategy. In 2000, James joined the firm's strategy committee and in 2002 he was elected to the firm's council.

At that time, Herbert Smith had no formal induction programmes or other methods of teaching the firm's vision, culture or values. Lawyers were supposed to absorb these things "by ESP". Together with Jonathan Scott, James's predecessor as senior partner, and Gavin Davies, who had recently returned from a secondment to Cravath, Swaine & Moore in New York, James helped put together an induction programme for trainees and new partners. He believes that the key advice for young lawyers is "believe in yourself".

Because we wouldn't have recruited you unless you were good enough. There's the self-starters, like me, but there's a lot of people who are cleverer than me and who don't realise they've got it. And so I really believe we have to give people the self-belief that our judgement of their abilities is good. So that's lesson one for a big group of them.

And the second thing I say is, seek out responsibility. Just do things you don't know how to do, don't be frightened of failing. And I always tell them, the story of my career is a story of learning from failure. It's about human beings. Bertrand Russell is one of my heroes; he writes about human weakness, failure and fallibility. His thesis is that is until you understand human beings are flawed, and we can fail, and are not that sophisticated, you can't enjoy life.

And that has been my philosophy throughout life. You do your best. You learn from things, you beat yourself up about the odd thing, but you have to be willing to fail. You pitch for a client and you don't win. Well, if you can't cope with that you can't be successful. You misread a situation. Well, who in life hasn't done that numerous times? But the truth is that [the young lawyers] hear it from us, and they like it. But they actually absorb the culture from the team they're in – not what they hear from on high.

James says that lawyers should always start from the truth. His father told him that if he didn't know the answer to a question, he should say so. Then, when he did offer an opinion, the client would know to take him seriously. In any situation, James would begin by stepping back and establishing the core facts and principles. He has been laughed at for this, but he does not mind.

Leading from the front

In around 2006, James became a group head, running a team of up to eight corporate partners. He also played a major part in developing the firm's capital markets practice but without a formal title. In 2010 he became head of corporate, an elected position for which he stood unopposed. He worked alongside a managing partner for corporate and spent most of his time doing client work. Looking back, he says that he failed to achieve most of the goals he had set himself for that role. He wanted more profitability than they ever achieved, and he wanted the firm to be even more market centric. James says he learned "a hell of a lot" by not achieving his goals and in some ways that taught him more than his successes.

I've been comfortable with failure, going back to when I failed my grade one music exam – and all 37 other people had passed! I think I have a greater fear of not trying. Lawyers who advise the clients never to take risk haven't understood context.

James believes that leaders have to lead. They have to back and support people but sometimes, on important things, they have to take difficult decisions and then be accountable for the consequences. Someone has to make a call, and law firms can be very indecisive organisations.

James went on the law firm leadership course at Harvard and returned with an abiding belief in the importance of execution.

> *For law firm leaders, issues are not usually about strategy. Any reasonably intelligent person can analyse a market and work out what's happening. The issues are in execution. People don't change because you urge them to change, it doesn't work. And I see a lot of law firm leadership that is standing on high, promulgating what should happen in the belief that the Red Sea will part.*
>
> *And that was the thing I learned at Harvard, and also from my tenure as head of corporate, when I'd set out some very clear goals, and I had set out some pretty clear thoughts on how we should execute on them. And the execution didn't happen. I think execution is where law firms are poor. We need to empower people. We know they are very smart people who can't be treated like cogs in a wheel. They're very obsessed with their intellect and ability and their rights. And they're the right person to judge how to advise the client, if they're out in the market they're going to be the right person to judge what the market opportunities are.*
>
> *But sometimes we need to just step in and say, "I know we talked about this, I know half of you agree and half of you don't, I tell you what, I may be wrong, but we're doing it". And this is how it is and I apologise if I'm proved wrong. Sometimes we do try something that is wrong. But trying is better than never trying. And we also know that usually lawyers are very, very good at dissecting the weaknesses of something new which is presented to them, because that's what they've had decades of training in. I think almost all firms have underinvested in management training for everyone.*

Balancing business and life

James is very aware of mental health issues, which were brought home to him through the personal experience of people close to him.

> *I am a typical lawyer. I don't understand anything until it's stuck in front of my nose. Mental health was stuck in front of my nose and I've become obsessed about it ever since. I've tried to role-model doing things that build resilience. So, for example, now I exercise, having not done it for years. I try to take an interest in people, ask how they are, and make sure that partners are aware of pressure*

points and ensuring people in their teams take their holidays. I'm on people's case about transition plans, about whether they have enough support. I am very passionate about it, actually. This is a complicated subject but I think as leaders we have a responsibility to try to challenge existing assumptions of what is healthy and acceptable for our teams. People make mistakes about how they treat other people in all organisations, almost always through ignorance, but I think culture on workplace health can and will change significantly.

Like many other law firm leaders, I worried a lot in late February and March 2020. I'm not embarrassed about it. I was worried about the firm then, because I had no idea what COVID was going to do. For example, if you lose 30% of your revenue, with fixed costs, you're in trouble. And you can be the strongest firm in the world. Whatever your margin, if that were to happen to you, you're in a pickle. So given we had no idea what would happen, we went hell for leather and put various measures in place to keep the firm financially resilient – Justin D'Agostino, our CEO elect, led this and really got into it. But I did have nights where I was waking six times, stewing about that. And that's very unusual for me. Of course, the actual outcome during COVID has been quite the opposite of what

"I love helping clients with complex issues. It's a privilege to get invited into boardrooms, to deal with organisations' most complicated problems."

we feared as it has been incredibly busy. But the other thing that really worries me on behalf of our firm and all firms, is I think there's an underestimation among many people of cyber risk. We all know that there are people who can hack anything and society has not fully resolved those risks.

James remains "ridiculously driven and energised" about "just doing law" and his interest extends well beyond fee-earning:

I love helping clients with complex issues. It's a privilege to get invited into boardrooms, to deal with organisations' most complicated problems. And I'm a bit of a nerd as well. I've written academically. From that weak academic background, I've sort of faked myself. I teach a seminar every year at Cambridge. And I love doing that. I'm also very involved in public policy; I chaired the City of London Law Society Company Law Committee and I chaired the takeover group for 14 years. I chaired an FCA panel, which is not a lawyer group, it's a practitioner group. I've sat on the FCA Markets Panel with CEOs and chairmen and such like. And I chair a think tank called Reform. It's deals with non-party political public policy; I love that stuff. And I can juggle a bit, as I've done for years. I did it long before I became senior partner.

But my biggest driver, and this is going to sound very boy-scoutish but it's the truth of my philosophy, is that I want to be proud of what I've done. I want people to feel that I've helped contribute. And I know I'll have failed thousands of times because the more authority you have, the more screw-ups you make, but I want to help give people careers that are a good part of their lives, and to deliver legal advice that helps the world tick – because businesses are just people really, just complicated groups of people. And I do think that business law is too often looked at as a way of making money. Our job is to help people do useful things in the world. And if we lose sight of that, and we think our job is to make money, we're going to get squashed because that's just dumb. It's not sustainable. And I'm actually quite positive because most law firm leaders I talk to feel pretty similarly.

People are motivated by a desire for autonomy. That doesn't mean a desire to be a partner in a law firm. It means a desire to have a degree of control and input into what they do. And to have a skill that they're proud of and they can develop and use. And to have a purpose to do something useful with others for someone else. I think those are the core motivators of most people, as the writer Dan Pink has said.

The Australian dimension

In 2012 Herbert Smith merged with Freehills, a leading Australian firm with over 190 partners and 800 lawyers. James championed the merger. He thought that Herbert Smith was international, but not nearly as international as some of its competitors. He thought it was about global positioning. "You need to be a market leader in more than one country" and Australia is a "serious high-quality market with brilliant lawyers". The merger meant that the Herbert Smith lockstep remuneration structure had to change, which was not without its difficulties, but the two firms had many shared values and a similar culture which made it a good fit.

James is "a huge fan" of the merger:

> *Communication and proximity create challenges. But I think if the model is eventually globalisation around the Americas, Europe, Asia, Africa, you have got to find ways of making it work. And I think it's very easy never to change, and to miss your opportunities to change your model. So that is why I was a big fan of it. And I have no regrets about it. And I think it did reposition Herbert Smith Freehills.*

Advice to a senior or managing partner

Distilling and summarising James's advice to new senior or managing partners is not difficult.

- Start with the truth.
- Give a lead and don't be afraid to make decisions.
- Focus on execution.

James Palmer
Partner, Herbert Smith Freehills
james.palmer@hsf.com

James Palmer was chair and senior partner at Herbert Smith Freehills from 2015 to April 2021, when he returned to full-time client focus following his second term in the role. He has been at the firm for 34 years, working from London and more briefly Hong Kong. He focuses on public and private M&A, capital markets, governance, foreign investment and financial regulatory work. As well as advising clients on these and on strategic and regulatory issues, he has had a long-standing involvement in development of business law and regulation.

He chaired the City of London Law Society's (CLLS) Company Law Committee from 2002 to 2006, during the development and introduction into law of the Companies Act 2006, and led the CLLS's expert takeovers group for 14 years, until 2015. From 2008–2020 he was a member of Financial Services Authority/Financial Conduct Authority panels on wholesale market issues, chairing one panel for six years. He is closely involved in policy issues for financial and professional services including through TheCityUK, where he also chairs the Legal Services Group. James is chair of Reform, a non-party think tank working to make public services better and smarter.

© Bill Knight

Kathleen Russ

Senior partner, Travers Smith LLP

Kathleen Russ is the senior partner of Travers Smith LLP, a London-based, City law firm which was founded in 1810. Travers Smith regularly acts on UK and cross-border matters, transactions and disputes, and is particularly well regarded for its pre-eminent expertise in asset management, M&A, disputes and investigations.

Early years

Kath was born in Nigeria and brought up in Fiji, where she attended school in "an extremely multicultural environment". Her parents were founding academics at the Open University, where their philosophy was "education for all". Kath's mother has always worked and has become one of the world's leading social anthropologists. Kath says that when she came back to the UK from Fiji, she went to a pretty tough state school in England and then joined the sixth form at one of the smartest private schools in the country. Learning to navigate and understand the environment in both school systems is something that Kath believes was instrumental in the development of her personality and values.

She read history at Mansfield College, Oxford. It was expected that she would go to Oxbridge: both her parents went to Oxford and her sisters went to Cambridge. Sport is important – Kath played hockey for Oxford, taking part in the Varsity Match with her sister on the Cambridge team. Both her sons have played badminton for England and Kath and her husband regularly compete in ultra marathons together (albeit very slowly).

Kath says that she did not work as hard at university as she might have done (although she did still receive an upper second), but she is proud of Mansfield College, which accepts around 95% of its intake from state schools, and now she is involved in its development. At university she was not entirely sure what she wanted as a career, but she had always wondered about law, in part because of the inspiration of her father who is a constitutional specialist. She did know that she wanted to continue studying and so law seemed a natural progression. She had a good CV and she had been told that the best people were working in the City, so it seemed natural to apply for articles there. She liked her interview with Travers Smith. Other firms had given her an easy ride, but Travers Smith gave her a hard time, and at the end of it she felt that she had been properly tested, and passed, and that they thought she would fit their culture. So she accepted and started work at the firm in 1991.

Kath had never worked in an office before and remembers finding it difficult to speak into her dictaphone in front of the partner she shared an office with. She was obliged to wear a skirt rather than trousers. She qualified into the tax department and there she stayed.

> *One of the hardest decisions I took was working out where I best fitted. And I say that because I was just as interested in corporate: I really, really enjoyed – and still enjoy – the dynamics and adrenaline of the deal. And I was quite tempted with the idea of becoming a corporate lawyer. But equally what I've always loved*

> *about tax is the really deep intellectual thinking that you have to do. You have to stay ahead of the legislation. It's very research based. And so ultimately, I decided that tax worked well, because I could do some of that really complex thinking, combining that with the adrenaline of the deal. My role has always been a tax lawyer on transactions, where my skill is to be able to understand in detail all of the legislation and the case law, and to be able to put that in the context of a commercial dynamic, and to be able to explain it in a language that my clients, who are mostly not tax people, will understand.*

From her time as an associate she remembers two things:

> *The first was that I had both of my children before I became a partner. And trying to reconcile the requirements of my children and motherhood with being a deal lawyer, was a constant challenge. And the second thing was the huge support that I had from one tax partner in particular, Rick Stratton, who had the ability to see the strength of different people who didn't fit the mould and went out of his way to nurture that and to build my belief in myself and my ability to continue to be successful at the firm.*

"Like I say to a lot of my young partners who now come through into the partnership, it is a really important stepping stone, but you should not imagine that you need to know everything when you suddenly become a partner, which is the expectation I placed on myself back then."

When she was an associate, Kath tried life outside the firm. Her husband took a job in Southampton and she tried working there, but she quickly realised that transactional tax lawyers "can't do it in Southampton", so came back to London.

The path to partnership

When Kath came back from her second period of maternity leave, no one had told her that she was on the partnership track.

One of the things about Travers back then was that nobody really talked about whether you were on partnership track or whether you wanted it. We thought that appraisals weren't about talking about your ambitions or your prospects – they were just to talk about your performance. And so I remember coming back from having my second son and being sat down and told that I was being put forward for partnership without any consultation as to whether I wanted it. But it did feel like a culmination of my ambitions. And I do remember being incredibly proud. But I also remember finding it quite difficult in the early years, because of the extra responsibility that it gave. And like I say to a lot of my young partners who now come through into the partnership, it is a really important stepping stone, but you should not imagine that you need to know everything when you suddenly become a partner, which is the expectation I placed on myself back then.

In those days the key responsibility was to take the ultimate decision on sometimes some very, very big and complex tax issues. And that, I think, was the thing that I found hardest because of course, before you become a partner, there's always an expectation that you would take a view, but then the final sign-off is by the partner. And I think I had this expectation on myself that when I became a partner I had to make all of those decisions myself, rather than being able to lean on all of my other partners to talk about these things with them. So I think the responsibility that I felt back then was very much around delivery to the clients on difficult judgement calls.

I think now what is expected of partners is so much more than that. It's not just the delivery to the client on a standalone mandate, it's to develop the business, it's to nurture our people, it's to exemplify our values, and our culture – all of those things. But I think back then, I did not feel those responsibilities, I felt the responsibility was more to deliver on the mandates that were given to me. And I think that was probably partly a function of how our department was at that time. It was more a support function for others rather than being a department that was building its own client base. And we changed that over time, including when I took over running the

> *department and we became very different. We became one of the firm's most successful business areas. Travers' tax department is disproportionately large compared to most other tax practices. Many of them have been retrenching, whereas we've been actively growing and have been a core part of the business.*

As she became more senior, Kath started to play an active part in tax outside the practice. She became a member of the British Venture Capital Association Tax Committee:

> *And that, for me was a really interesting new role that I was doing, because it wasn't just doing the client work, I was out there really being actively involved with the Revenue and the Treasury in terms of shaping policy. And that was fascinating, but also gave me a real insight into the importance of horizon scanning for clients and really thinking about what trends are coming up and helping clients to prepare for that, rather than just dealing with what is on the agenda now. So I think the Committee role was very important in helping shape me as a client-facing partner, but also helping to build my profile in the City.*

Kath ran the tax department at the firm from 2007 to 2017. Her work outside the firm has led to a position on the board of the Office of Tax Simplification, providing advice to the Chancellor on simplifying the UK tax system. She is also a member of the CBI London Regional Council.

The move to management

While she was running the tax department, Kath was elected to the management committee of the firm. In 2017, she chose to stand down as head of the tax department in support of the firm's presumption that nobody should head a department for more than two terms. In 2019, she became senior partner.

> *I give a lot of credit to other partners in the firm for pushing me to stand. I'm not as confident as some people are; maybe no one's as confident as they seem to be on the surface. I don't always believe in myself the way I should. I would not have put myself forward for either the management committee or to be our senior partner, without people really pushing me to do that. And in this particular case, there were a couple of partners who started talking to me a good few years before I put myself forward for the management committee. And in the end I decided that I did want to stand, but I would still say that standing for the management committee – and ultimately, as senior partner – was incredibly difficult for me, because I knew that if you put yourself forward in that way that you could fail, and I hate failure. So I did find it very difficult to do it. But I decided that I really wanted to. And I was lucky that I was*

"[It] gave me a real insight into the importance of horizon scanning for clients and really thinking about what trends are coming up and helping clients to prepare for that, rather than just dealing with what is on the agenda now."

elected the first time I stood as a member of management committee. And then once I did it, I just enjoyed it. When I get stuck into something, and I enjoy it, then I want more.

As senior partner, Kath devotes 20% of her time to fee-earning work and the rest to her role as an ambassador for the firm and also in chairing the firm's partnership board, audit committee and diversity and inclusion and environmental boards. The firm's current managing partner is David Patient, who will be succeeded by Edmund Reed from July 2021, and Kath believes that it is important for the senior partner and managing partner to work together in a way which suits their personalities and approach. She expects that she will work with Edmund differently from the way in which she works with David.

Kath says that Travers Smith has a growth strategy, but no intention to grow overseas. A key point is to remain independent – not connected with a formal international network and, by using this model, to be nimble in responding to the clients' needs worldwide through an appropriate and efficient use of this network. The firm is very keen to be best in class in the sectors that they choose, but they don't want to be all things to all clients: they prefer to be selective in the work they do, and where they choose to do it. They choose to do their work "in an absolutely market-leading way and not to do it otherwise". The core pillars of the firm are asset management, M&A, and disputes and investigations.

Kath talks to all the trainees when they first arrive about her experiences as a young lawyer and what they should think about during their career.

> *I tell trainees to believe in themselves – to recognise that it's OK to make mistakes, because a career is about always learning and not believing that you have to know everything in the beginning. I tell them that trust and integrity are completely non-negotiable, but beyond that they're here to learn and develop rather than only to be a resource.*

The biggest change that Kath has seen in her time is an acknowledgement that a lawyer is a whole person – not just a lawyer. Accepting that we all come with baggage is the right thing to do.

> *You would have been told, never, ever tell your clients that you can't do a call because you're picking your kids up from school. And actually, I don't think that's the culture now. A lot of the clients that we now work with, I think, give us more work because they know we're interesting people with the same life challenges that they have, rather than being just a lawyer.*

"A lot of the clients that we now work with, I think, give us more work because they know we're interesting people with the same life challenges that they have, rather than being just a lawyer."

Diversity and inclusion

This is a subject very close to Kath's heart. She believes that her childhood in Fiji and her mixed education in England taught her to understand the potential of different people.

> *Diversity and inclusion is absolutely integral to the success of any law firm. I think if you want to have the best people work for you, they come from myriad backgrounds and not from one particular area. I also think that unless you've got properly diverse people within your organisation, you will not have a diverse set of clients, and it would be completely wrong to believe that the clients we want to act for are all white middle-class men. So it's always been my view that we need to have a real range of talent within the firm. In my own department, before D&I was something that people talked about, I just had a natural instinct of wanting to nurture the potential of people from all sorts of different backgrounds. I didn't badge that as diversity and inclusion back then, I would just have badged it as wanting the best people and being open-minded as to who those best people are. And I was very much led by Rick Stratton, who looked at me and saw something very different in me and really pushed me when I was young. And I tried to be open-minded in the same way to others coming up behind me. Our department now has more female than male partners and an excellent gender mix in the talent pipeline. I know that some of that has to do with me and the way that I had approached talent. So that was sort of what I was doing almost in my whole career as head of tax department without realising I was doing it.*
>
> *Travers was not good on this in the early years of my career; it was old fashioned. It was dominated by white men; the attitudes to women were not particularly progressive. We had nobody who was openly gay, nor a good mix of ethnicities. It was not a progressive place. And I definitely had a lot of times when, as a female partner, I was extremely uncomfortable in the environment. So I was surrounded by a culture where I was definitely "other" as opposed to part of the norm. And it did make it very challenging, and I questioned myself a lot more than I think I would otherwise have done.*

Kath did get to the top. She says that she never suffered from discrimination, but she found it hard all the way through. She realised that if her experience was anything to go by, then lots of other people were finding it challenging too and it became her "driving determination" to create a culture where Travers Smith didn't just recruit the best, but also retained the best – a wide range of different people from different backgrounds. As an example, when she became senior partner, well before the Black Lives Matter movement, she put at the forefront of her agenda doing more to try to improve the firm's record in recruiting and retaining those from black and minority ethnic backgrounds. She thinks that is the right thing to do, not only ethically and morally, but also because it is "absolutely key" to the firm's future success.

What practical steps does she take to further diversity and inclusion?

> *First of all, it's important that the senior leadership talks about this the whole time. Also very much acknowledging and remembering that me talking about these things, and David talking about these things, is only a third of the way to making progress. The next thing you've got to do is enact things within the organisation which facilitate that progress. And the final thing you've got to do is crack the experience that people are having. I think that too often firms focus on the slogans and the statements externally and internally, and they forget that you can say whatever you want, but if the experience on the ground is not the same, then you haven't really achieved what you want to achieve.*
>
> *So a lot of what I've done is focused on the internal experience of people and whether that reflects the culture that we are seeking to espouse, and a lot of that is around winning the hearts and the minds of senior people in our firm. And then getting them to ensure that those philosophies are shared by the partners and then by their teams, because that's what really changes the experience of people. So to give you an example, we are looking hard at work allocation, which has all sorts of different things that feed off it. Obviously, profitability for the firm – that's obviously key – it's effective utilisation. But it also has all sorts of implications from a D&I angle. If you choose a client team by reference to "fit", that may have meant choosing someone who enjoys playing golf or watching rugby with a client. But if so, you're not giving a fair opportunity to others from different backgrounds who could otherwise get those opportunities and increase their prospects of becoming the partners of the future.*
>
> *And if you've got people who want to do more work from home, how do you ensure that you still bring them into some of the really important client mandates of the future, notwithstanding the fact that they're working from home? If you've got somebody who is Jewish who can't work on a Friday afternoon when deals may often be signing, how do you ensure that you don't take them out of really important relationships?*

Kath says that when a woman comes back from maternity leave, it too often happens that people in the City, not just men, assume she wants to prioritise her children and therefore count her out from some of the most difficult and time-consuming mandates. In her view, that is "coming from the right place" because people are trying to ensure that the woman is not overburdened. But if the returning employee is denied that opportunity, she may not become a partner; if you give those same opportunities to a man, then he is more likely to do so. So Kath encourages all leaders to talk to a woman in that situation about what she wants. She may say, as Kath did, that she wants the same opportunities as any other lawyer would have, and she will decide how to manage her children. Or she may request a lighter workload as she wants to prioritise her kids, but the firm cannot take that decision for her. It must be the employee's decision alone.

Taking action on the environment

Kath is also very concerned about the firm's approach to environmental issues.

> *If you ask me what the big things are coming down the pipeline for our clients, it's all around climate change and carbon, and it's an opportunity as well as a necessity for us to be involved in that. So being visible on it, understanding the trends, thinking about what's coming, is a very important part of what I do from a*

> *"A lot of what I've done is focused on the internal experience of people and whether that reflects the culture that we are seeking to espouse, and a lot of that is around winning the hearts and the minds of senior people in our firm."*

business development perspective. But on the other side of it, we have responsibilities as a business to ensure that we are thinking about our own impact on the environment. And so I've been focused hard on thinking about what our own responsibilities are – what we can ourselves change, whether that's on business travel, whether it's on how we run our kitchen, and using sustainable products, whether it's not using too much paper – all of those things. We're also focused on the fact that we can influence our suppliers because we have buying power. We may not be as big as Linklaters and Freshfields, but we do have buying power, and we're trying to use our buying power to influence our suppliers and get them to sign up to some of the key commitments around this as well.

We're also acknowledging that as lawyers, leading lawyers, we've got great legal expertise that can help drive change in this area. And so we're quite actively involved in working with some of the environmental charities who need legal advice and giving that to them on a pro bono basis. So what can lawyers do best? We can go off and give money to charities and so on. And we obviously do all of that. But what's the unique thing that we can give – it's legal expertise. So where can we make the most changes by using that expertise in the areas which are needed?

"I aspire for Travers Smith to be best in class, in all that we choose to do. That, in a nutshell, is how I see my role at the firm."

Values drive value

Kath emphasises that, when looking at issues around D&I, the environment or the firm's culture, the values of the firm matter. They matter to all relevant stakeholders, whether clients, prospective clients, suppliers, intermediaries, partners or employees. In her capacity as senior partner, these issues also matter hugely to Kath. She is, after all, the custodian of the firm's values. But she also strongly believes that values drive value. And it is in that context that these issues need to be considered. Travers Smith is a highly respected London law firm and one of the few truly independent firms of its type. It focuses on working on highly complex areas of law for large, often high-profile, always sophisticated clients. It is a very successful business and, as senior partner, Kath's focus is on all aspects of its success. Perhaps in view of her sporting background, Kath acknowledges she is extremely competitive. "I aspire for Travers Smith to be best in class, in all that we choose to do. That, in a nutshell, is how I see my role at the firm."

Advice to a managing or senior partner

- Spend as much time thinking about what should be on your future agenda as you do about your current agenda.
- Do not be afraid to take risks.
- Be brave enough to take decisions.

Kathleen Russ
Senior partner, Travers Smith LLP
kathleen.russ@traverssmith.com

Kathleen Russ was elected as Travers Smith's senior partner in 2019, having been partner in the tax department since 2001, and head of the tax department for almost ten years, growing it into one of the firm's key business areas. She is regarded as one of the City's leading tax advisers with long-standing experience advising on complex transactions in the alternative asset management sector. She was a member of the BVCA Tax Committee between 2002–17 and now sits on the board of the Office of Tax Simplification as a non-executive director, providing advice to the Chancellor on simplifying the UK tax system.

As senior partner, Kathleen occupies a strategic and leadership role in the firm and chairs both the partnership board and the audit committee. She also chairs the Travers Smith boards which have responsibility for diversity and inclusion and the environment, with those roles reflecting the importance that she ascribes to those issues.

© Bill Knight

Victoria Sampson and Joseph Oates

Partners, CooperBurnett LLP

Victoria Sampson and Joseph (Joe) Oates share the management of CooperBurnett LLP, a four-partner full-service law firm in Tunbridge Wells, Kent, employing 20+ lawyers. The firm changed dramatically from 2014 to 2016 when a number of partners retired, including Jonathan Smithers, who was president of the Law Society of England and Wales. Victoria and Joe have been running the firm ever since and are about to launch their new strategy.

Early years

Joe

Joe read history at Lancaster University and then completed a master's at the London School of Economics. He decided upon law as he understood its practice would mirror, to an extent, an academic approach which he enjoyed at university. Having undertaken various placements in London firms, Joe knew that he would prefer close contact with clients and colleagues and so found training at Dean Wilson, a Brighton firm, ideal. Joe enjoyed litigation during training.

Joe took away some important lessons from Dean Wilson:

> *I liked the collegiate atmosphere. I liked the fact that if you demonstrate a confidence and a level of competence, you're able to get on with stuff. One hears of bigger firms clocking in, clocking out, working until 11pm, quite impersonal and target driven. Having a freedom to be able to perceive what you found interesting and look for your own clients. I found that good, and it's replicated here.*

Joe joined CooperBurnett in 1999 after another lawyer introduced him to Nigel Burnett, then the senior partner of the firm. He quickly became part of the firm's management and joined the managing committee with Nigel Burnett and Jonathan Smithers in 2003. Joe is also a licensed insolvency practitioner, being only one of a handful of solicitors holding dual qualification.

Victoria

Victoria attended South Bank University in London, followed by law school in Bristol. When she was 11, she told her parents she was going to be a solicitor. There were no lawyers in the family, but her father was in the insurance industry and through him Victoria had been exposed enough to media and commercial law to whet her appetite. In her teens she followed cases involving miscarriages of justice, such as the Guildford and Birmingham IRA pub bombings. She was always going to be a lawyer and she read law at university as a means to an end.

Victoria joined CooperBurnett when she was 23 in April 1996. She had been working as a paralegal in London, but it felt "too anonymous".

> *I just remember it was open plan, lots of elevators and people not talking. I'm very much a people person. I needed to get into the guts of things and get on with stuff.*

Victoria got her training contract when her mother, who was selling the family house, told the estate agent that her daughter wanted to be a solicitor. The agent had a good relationship with CooperBurnett and Victoria found herself being interviewed that afternoon.

Victoria is a corporate and commercial lawyer. For the last nine months of her training, she sat with Nigel Burnett doing commercial work.

> *He involved me in every single meeting that occurred with commercial clients. And having joined the firm thinking I wanted to help people I realised that I was never going to be a litigator, I was never going to do the contentious side of life; I have always been a non-contentious lawyer, and I loved the commercial corporate world. I was given every opportunity to get into the belly of the Tunbridge Wells business community and beyond. There was a lot of lending going on at that time, so we had associations with lots of banks, and we were doing a lot of financing and so on. I qualified in 1998 and it just went from there, really. I thoroughly, thoroughly enjoyed what I was doing, and those very long hours that I wanted to do, although it was demanding. It seems a long time ago now!*

"It doesn't matter which firm you're in, it's what you're doing for your clients and for their business."

Qualification and partnership

After qualification Victoria was free to develop her practice.

> *You go to bed as a trainee, you wake up the next day as a qualified solicitor, which is just peculiar. We had complete autonomy to go out and carve our own niche, which now from a risk perspective makes me think "Oh, my gosh", but at that time that's what we were encouraged to do. And we were told, "Act like a trainee partner". And that's what I did. John Tickner was one of my mentors. He just had such a depth about him, and was so considered. Whatever happened, there would always be a solution. Our practice manager at the time, Judith Slater, was very matriarchal. She'd been in the firm pretty much since 1981, when it was formed. She was also a mentor. She taught me that people were so important. She'd listen to everybody, and she'd really fuse people together. And she always knew what to do, as well. Later Jonathan Smithers, former president of the Law Society, showed me that when people looked at our business – you know, a firm in Tunbridge Wells – it doesn't matter which firm you're in, it's what you're doing for your clients and for their business.*

Joe also believes in autonomy. When he is talking to young lawyers, he tries to pass on what he has benefited from.

> *We love them to work hard, and we love them not to feel as if every single day, every week, they're having to account for every ounce of time. And I think that we deliver that message by, for example, not being overly focused on chargeable hours. Although it's difficult for Victoria and me to know, because we haven't really worked elsewhere, we do find when people join us that they consider it to be a freer atmosphere in terms of their economic performance. Partly, I think it's because we've got confidence in who we recruit. We expect dedication, enthusiasm and commitment, but that doesn't have to demonstrate itself in certain criteria that we impose on them. You can tell it at the end of the month, and at the end of the year, and they know that we recognise it.*

Victoria and Joe became partners in 2001 and 2002 respectively and continued to develop their practices as working lawyers. The partnership then was like "a group of GPs". There was a management committee, with a senior partner (Nigel Burnett), a managing partner (Jonathan Smithers) and Joe, which took financial decisions and managed the firm day to day but there was no plan to develop the firm. Nobody was thinking about how the firm was going to look in five years' time.

Running the show

Then from 2014 to 2016 four equity partners retired, leaving Victoria and Joe as two of the three equity partners remaining in the firm. Until then, Joe and Victoria had not worked together much but now they were "obliged" to. Joe remembers:

> *We had already conceived that there would be no replication of what existed previously in terms of senior partner, managing partner and myself in the managing committee. So when everybody else had gone we knew instinctively, and then verbalised, that we wouldn't be replicating the management because we knew it wasn't just Victoria and me: we wanted to reach out to colleagues within the firm, who in a more traditional setting had been overlooked.*

Victoria picks up the story:

> *It's empowerment, essentially, and recognition of people's worth and value to the firm, without any fear whatsoever, and we embraced it. We had some challenges which we dealt with, and in a very short time, we've made quite a lot of difference to the firm, I believe in a very good and meaningful way. At the moment, we're actively recruiting, and really trying to bring the firm forward. We're going to be launching a plan which comes down to three Ps, and one of them isn't 'pandemic'. But it's almost born of the pandemic because that really forced us to look at our business in a way that we wouldn't necessarily have if the whole country hadn't locked down in March 2020.*

Joe continues:

> *We recognised that we had an absence of that commitment to future development, partly because we're a successful firm. And it was enough for previous equity partners just to be successful, but not to think about where we might like to be in five or ten years' time. We recognised that people within the firm, although they may be feeling well rewarded, also want to feel excited and enthused. And that's certainly a way of retaining people.*

Strategy

Victoria explains the plan:

> *So the first P is for 'people'. Our objective is to retain and attract the best possible people to our team. Retention and attraction are two different things, but equally exciting. The second P is also 'people'. And that is retaining and attracting the best people to work with – our clients and contacts. With the best people, we*

"We recognised that people within the firm, although they may be feeling well rewarded, also want to feel excited and enthused. And that's certainly a way of retaining people."

can attract the best people and retain the best clients and the best referrals. And the third P is 'profit'. And so from the first two Ps, we will be more profitable, and our virtuous circle will keep feeding itself. So the firm will be benefiting, and we will be rewarding and incentivising and motivating all of our first P. And it goes on and on and on. And when we say it out loud, it sounds incredibly simple. But for our firm, it is incredibly exciting. And we've demonstrated our commitment since February 2020 in terms of our recruitment. We've taken on seven new lawyers over the last nine months. And we have addressed and embraced flexibility and remote working – all of the things that we've been forced into doing to a degree, but realising we can make this business utterly brilliant. Can I say that?

I'm excited because I know that once I get started, I get very passionate about the business. I've loved my career, and I've loved what I've done. But I've never been challenged in this way before. And to co-lead and to bring the firm forward and to bring people with us in a way that is exciting. It's brilliant for us.

Joe is more cautious:

I don't expect to have a level of interest or passion about work in the way that Victoria has, partly this results from my long-standing

> *involvement in risk and compliance for the firm which, by necessity, sometimes involves challenging internal decision making in the firm's interests. This has contrasted with Victoria's focus on external relations and business development, at which she excels. While we maintain our broad internal/external bias to our leadership roles, I can say in the last three or four years it has certainly been more interesting, because we've been able to change it up and bring in people who would not have been brought in before, to consult with us, to be involved and to contribute and I've enjoyed that. For example, Gareth Warner, who heads our accounts team, has been here since the year dot, working his way all the way up to the top, and knows about the firm from a different perspective to us. So he's involved in our equity partners' meetings. Jenni Irving, head of residential property, who similarly has worked all the way up to the top, is involved as well. And that would have been inconceivable previously, due to the hierarchical structure. And that's been fun, if that's the word.*

Joe and Victoria are clear that they want to run their firm as a business and to discuss issues such as profit openly, to ensure that everyone knows what they must do to improve profitability and that they will be rewarded if they succeed. They believe that they get good

"We've been able to change it up and bring in people who would not have been brought in before, to consult with us, to be involved and to contribute and I've enjoyed that."

results from empowering people – for example, they believe that the firm's social media presence stands out among the local firms because they have entrusted the Instagram account to an enthusiastic employee in the residential conveyancing department.

Communicating the plan during the pandemic is going to raise problems of its own. As Victoria explains:

> *Well, we had obviously wanted a face-to-face meeting, but we can't have one at the moment. Everything's gearing up to our ruby anniversary in April 2021. We're 40 years old then which is not old to some, but for us it's something to celebrate. And I think it's a launchpad for us. And we're going to launch the plan then.*
>
> *It's all very well doing Zoom or Teams or whatever, but nothing beats seeing people in person and being able to feed off their reactions and read the room – understanding how people are reacting to what you're saying. And we're going to need to work out how we're going to do that in a very impactful way because we want them to buy into it, don't we? It will come, but the thing is, what we can't do is give them kind of false messages, not false messages but hollow messages, which have no meat, because it could just be perceived as air. So we need to think very carefully about remuneration in a way that we haven't done before. Because we've been very instinctive, haven't we, in terms of how we've remunerated people?*

The solicitor's role

Joe and Victoria take advice about management from their accountants, from friends in the business community and from their clients. IT is very important as the firm adapts to remote working. Email changes relationships with clients. Quick-fire communication goes back and forth without formality. Traditional notions of the solicitor being a remote representative of a learned profession are bound to change. As Joe explains:

> *In fact, many of our best lawyers are people who don't have a formal qualification...*

Victoria sees things slightly differently:

> *At the end of the day, I respect someone who has worked bloody hard to get where they are, regardless of how they got there. And being a solicitor is still a profession, in my mind. And I think a lot of people still do respect a profession. I see some of my clients when they're exiting their business after doing 35 years or whatever, and they put on a shirt and tie to come to see me, and I'm going to*

> *"It's all very well doing Zoom or Teams or whatever, but nothing beats seeing people in person and being able to feed off their reactions and read the room – understanding how people are reacting to what you're saying. And we're going to need to work out how we're going to do that in a very impactful way because we want them to buy into it, don't we?"*

respect the fact that they respect that and that they've seen us as someone that's going to provide a service to them. Some clients will want to use us because we've got professional indemnity insurance. We know that. And we don't want to deal with those sorts of people; we want to deal with people where we can add value.

I deliberately took a path to get to where I am. And I've got no regrets whatsoever. I've absolutely loved what I've done. And it's given me the opportunity now, as a business owner, to do this. And this – this is amazing and exciting, and a real challenge.

Advice to a senior or managing partner

- Victoria says that you must listen – to your instincts, to your partners and to your people.
- Joe says that you must believe you have something to contribute. Don't do it just for money or position.
- They both agree that if you make a mistake, it's not the end of the world. If you have done it for the right reasons, you will learn from it.

Joseph Oates
Partner, CooperBurnett LLP
JMO@cooperburnett.com

Head of the Contentious Department at CooperBurnett, Joseph Oates joined the firm in 1999 and became a partner in 2002. He has been a member of the firm's management board since 2003, where he co-leads in the development and implementation of the firm's strategy and plan.

Joseph has over 20 years' experience in advising insolvency practitioners, business and individual clients on contentious and non-contentious matters. He has a thorough understanding of insolvency law and practice and successfully completed the Joint Insolvency Examination Board (JIEB) insolvency exams in 2009.

As a trained mediator, Joseph adopts a commercial and straightforward approach to resolving disputes and he advises on all aspects of contentious employment law, including settlement agreements.

In his spare time, Joseph is a keen footballer and has, more recently, taken to long cycle rides, having been part of the CooperBurnett team which rode from London to Paris in 24 hours in aid of Brain Tumour Research.

Victoria Sampson
Partner, CooperBurnett LLP
VLS@cooperburnett.com

Victoria Sampson is head of the Corporate and Commercial Services team at CooperBurnett. She has been with the firm for 25 years, having joined as a trainee in 1996. Victoria became a partner in 2001 and sits on the management board, co-leading in the development and implementation of the firm's strategy.

Victoria advises on all aspects of corporate and commercial law, including mergers and acquisitions, and enjoys supporting business owners. She works with shareholders, directors and partners in respect of all types of commercial contracts and regularly acts for banks and financial institutions in perfecting security, as well as advising them on corporate finance matters.

In addition to being president of West Kent Chamber of Commerce and Industry on two separate occasions, Victoria is an ambassador for the children's hospice charity, ellenor, and also joined colleagues to cycle from London to Paris in just 24 hours in aid of Brain Tumour Research.

© Sorainen

Aku Sorainen

Founder and senior partner, Sorainen

Aku Sorainen is the founder and senior partner of Sorainen, a 31-partner, 200-lawyer business law firm with offices in Estonia, Latvia, Lithuania and Belarus. Aku founded the firm in 1995 to take part in the rising prosperity of the region after the fall of communism.

Early years

Born in Finland, Aku read law at the University of Lapland. When he was 12 years old, he wanted to be an ambassador and he asked his father what he should do about that. His father suggested that he should call the Finnish Ministry of Foreign affairs, and they recommended that he should study law.

Aku went on study law but with the thought that he would be a businessman. In the late 1980s, he was studying in a summer programme at Humboldt University in East Berlin and could see the effects of communism at first hand. As a foreigner, he could visit the West to change his DDR Marks for Deutschmarks and live "like a king" in East Berlin on the proceeds. In July 1988, a Bruce Springsteen concert in East Berlin attracted over 300,000 people and ended in chaos. Aku could see that the system was not going to last. Sixteen months later, the Berlin Wall came down and Aku, then 26, went with his hammer to get a piece of it.

Two years later, when the Baltic countries became independent, Aku decided to write his master's thesis on the business laws of the emerging Baltic states. He interviewed academics, businessmen and officials and quickly realised that this was a major topic. He approached Finnish corporations for sponsorship and was surprised by the positive response. He received enough funding to enable him to live for a year and a half while completing his thesis.

Aku wrote his thesis in English, which was unusual at that time in Finland, and it was published as a book, attracting attention. Before long, Aku was receiving requests for advice from the general counsel of large corporations who wanted to do business in the region, and he realised that he had a unique opportunity to build a career. As soon as he graduated, he volunteered to go to Tallinn, Estonia, and set up a law office for a Finnish firm. This was a challenging time, as Aku had no training in the practical business of running an office or advising clients. His first clients were Finnish subsidiaries of corporations, such as ABB, the technology and infrastructure company, and he trained himself.

Founding Sorainen

In 1995 Aku borrowed a computer and printer from one of his clients, the gas company AGA, and set up his own firm in the Tallinn office with lawyers from the US, Sweden and Finland. He then found his first Estonian lawyer. Within six months, the firm employed seven lawyers. Managing the team was not easy, given their diverse backgrounds, but Aku brought his own values to these issues, tackling them with "what he had learned at home".

"Coming from Finland, it would be so much easier to lead a homogeneous organisation with people who have grown up and lived there too, but if you want to lead an international organisation, everything is different, and a kind of additional flavour is given by the fact that you are not a huge international corporation with very strong internal corporate culture."

It was quite a challenge in the beginning and remains so today. Management has so much to do with the culture and the values of people. Coming from Finland, it would be so much easier to lead a homogeneous organisation with people who have grown up and lived there too, but if you want to lead an international organisation, everything is different, and a kind of additional flavour is given by the fact that you are not a huge international corporation with very strong internal corporate culture. It's a different thing when General Electric or British Petroleum expands to different countries, they bring in a huge infrastructure.

There was no rule of law. It was real chaos. Bribes were normal in society and even in the courts. But reform came when these countries wanted to join the EU in the mid-90s. They took a clear direction towards meeting EU criteria and establishing the rule of law, and every year it was getting better and better.

Security in Estonia was lax. During Aku's firm's first year of business, 75 bombs went off in Tallinn. "Organised crime gangs even bombed the nearby police station," he explains. Today, Estonia is a member of the EU and NATO and it is difficult to imagine what it was like previously. "But," says Aku, "it was a lot of fun. There were a lot of positive things happening."

Developing the firm

Initially, all the lawyers worked in one room, which helped facilitate collaboration. After two years, Aku dispatched a Finnish law student to open an office in Riga, Latvia and another recent Finnish graduate to set up operations in Vilnius, Lithuania. His competitors were the local firms. Nobody else was trying to build a regional law firm.

> *Nobody believed in it. Because these countries still had different languages, they had decided to go in different directions with their legislation. They all came from the Soviet Union with the same legislation but from the early 1990s they went their own way. Estonia copied a lot of the legislation from Finland and Sweden, Latvia reintroduced legislation from before the Second World War, Lithuania tried to modernise the Soviet legislation and even copied ideas from Canada. It was a big mess. So nobody believed that there was any sense in trying to build a regional law firm covering these three Baltic countries.*
>
> *But I had done my thesis here a few years earlier, in the early 90s. So I knew a lot of people in these three countries. And I felt that eventually they would want to join the EU. And once they were in the EU, then they would be forced to harmonise. So I thought that even if they did go in different directions, it would only be temporarily.*

Although Aku started the Latvian and Lithuanian offices with Finnish lawyers, they did not become partners and had left the firm by the time Aku appointed the first local partners, first in Lithuania, and subsequently in Latvia and Estonia. His guiding principle was that these lawyers should share his values.

Aku was at the centre of things as the region developed. He has met all of Estonia's presidents and prime ministers:

> *Many of our clients had large projects already at that time and it was actually pretty easy to call the Prime Minister's office and say, "We have this big opportunity here. Would you like to meet us?"*

AI and IT

The Sorainen website emphasises the part IT plays in running the firm, but Aku is frank about its current limitations as well as its capabilities:

> *I wouldn't say AI makes a huge difference today. I think it is completely overrated, currently, for our business. It may start to make a difference for UK firms who have trained their systems in the English language, but we are using these very curious languages and these systems are not yet up to speed with them.*

AI is pretty useless. But obviously, it's good to have a very modern practice-management system so that you can find your templates and your client data easily. Without that, we wouldn't be here. And I see very good potential in other technology, like collaboration tools, clause libraries, enterprise search engines and document automation. We are making big steps forward there currently. Yesterday we launched an automated share-purchase agreement for three Baltic countries. We automated one master template, which combined 15 others. You just choose which country you want, start filling in the answers and a 30-page document is produced.

I think we invested 100 hours from three offices into preparing this. But I remember talking to one Magic Circle law firm partner just a couple of years ago in London, and I asked about the same tool and he said that, yes, they do see potential, but they had not been able to make a start [on developing one]. And I said, "If you want, you can invest millions into the system right away". And he said, "Yes, but the partners cannot agree on the terminology".

Recruitment and training

Sorainen started to provide litigation and dispute resolution once the Baltic systems became less corrupt and today they are a full-service

"I think that the firm's culture is getting stronger year by year, and one of its values is collaboration. It is about having a kind of friendly attitude to and relations with your peers and colleagues and co-workers and having a flat hierarchy where people can easily approach each other."

business law firm. Staff are recruited locally. In the beginning, it made sense to import expatriates because they had an understanding of the future for the Baltic region, but now Sorainen has established its own academy to offer practical training for law students – 20 to 25 every year from each country. The training is done in-house by Sorainen partners and associates. The firm picks the brightest and offers them training contracts when they graduate, but first they join the 'Sorainen Think Tank', where they are given assignments and have to decide amongst themselves who is best placed to handle them.

> *I think that the firm's culture is getting stronger year by year, and one of its values is collaboration. It is about having a kind of friendly attitude to and relations with your peers and colleagues and co-workers and having a flat hierarchy where people can easily approach each other. This culture is different from many other law firms in the market. People grow up in our system, and they learn to appreciate it, especially those who have worked somewhere else before. It's always a challenge with those young ones. We take them from university and grow them and they have not seen anything else. But they want to see the world, which is very natural for young people – they want to have different types of experiences. So we tend to lose many of them because they just want to see what it's like elsewhere.*

Culture and values

Aku leads the culture of the firm.

> *I try to lead the strategy of the firm and I see my role as leading the partnership. We have a very committed managing partner, Laimonas Skibarka, who is leading the operations and implementing the strategy. And we have various partner committees on different topics. Most of our partners are grown from inside the firm. That is the best way to ensure that we have the right culture; that new partners strengthen the corporate culture. And we have a process of starting new partners on the partner development track, which is a formal process usually for three years. And then these partner candidates get more mentoring and coaching, they get to make presentations to the whole partnership. And once they get closer to this promotion, then we have an election process where the whole partnership selects all the new partners.*

Aku says that the partners seldom vote but proceed by consensus. I suggest that as the founder of the firm which bears his name, his influence must be considerable. He shakes his head but when I suggest that any consensus must include him, he does not deny it.

He explains that COVID-19 has been a test of the firm's culture:

> *Last spring we had to cut costs throughout the firm and in all positions. We didn't lay off people, but we froze salaries; we cancelled training, travel, everything. And now as we are getting back to normal and we are budgeting for next year, many partners like the cuts. We will make a record profit this year. In early 2020, we feared for our revenue, but now it turns out that revenue is growing quite nicely. So this will be a great year – many partners like it and say: "This is a very lean organisation now that we have been able to cut all these costs; let's keep it the same next year."*
>
> *And I have said, this is against our culture. I mean, we can do it for one year, but if we cut these costs permanently, this will damage our culture. And then the question arose, what is our culture? Can you explain it? I made quite an effort to write it down. So next week we are going to discuss it with the partners. Do they agree with it, or do they want to change it? We hired a consultant to facilitate this discussion. I think it's better to have a professional to do that. I might be a bit biased myself…*
>
> *Maybe six, seven, eight years ago, we employed a consultant on billing, specifically, how to maximise it. And there was an interesting discussion later on in the firm and we didn't really agree. There were many good points, but we didn't agree on the principle of maximising the billing as such. We did not think it was in accordance with the firm's value on helping clients succeed in business. What we want is a win-win. We want to produce value for the clients and expect them to be ready to pay because we produce value. But that is a different approach to the one the consultant wanted.*

What significant moments have influenced Aku's career?

> *I've learned tough lessons, which have had a strong influence on my career, but they were not exactly moments. In my very first law firm, where I worked for two years, the leadership style of the named partner of that firm was an example of how not to treat people. I realised I would never want to work in that way.*
>
> *And I have had one very painful departure of one of the leading partners in my firm, which also taught me an important lesson about trusting people and then how to agree departures. It taught me that when trust starts to fall away, you should not let it go unnoticed. You should start to act.*

Aku believes that there is no substitute for professional skill. It is all very well being a great rainmaker with an attractive, outgoing

"In my very first law firm, where I worked for two years, the leadership style of the named partner of that firm was an example of how not to treat people. I realised I would never want to work in that way."

personality, but as the legal market matures, it is critical to do good work. People need first and foremost to be excellent lawyers.

I ask him about the difficulties of running the office in Belarus with the unrest caused by 2020's disputed election.

> *We have had many discussions about how we should act. Should we do something different given the current turmoil there? Should we somehow change our public profile? But we have decided to keep our head down, to continue working. Our core purpose is increasing prosperity in the Baltic states and Belarus by helping clients succeed in business. And this is also what we believe is the right thing. The more we help companies in business, that will also help the country to modernise.*
>
> *But indeed, these are very stressful times there, and also for our personnel on an individual basis. The high level of COVID-19 infections at the same time doesn't make it easier. Many of our competitors have been detained for, let's say, keeping a higher profile – a public profile on supporting these movements. And I don't think it's necessarily a good thing for the future of your firm if your partners are detained.*

Lessons learned

Drawing on over 20 years' experience in the Baltics, Aku says:

> *Managing a law firm is a full-time role if you have more than 50 lawyers. I think many managing partners make this mistake. They love servicing clients, and they think they can make management a part-time role. But if you do that, you just end up dealing with administrative things and fire-fighting, and you never really get into strategic leadership. I always think that if I invest one day of my time in helping clients' businesses, then it's one day away from building our own business. Of course, our lawyers and partners must be primarily client focused and I have a large responsibility in being primarily focused on our own business as it must constantly add value.*
>
> *You have to talk to everyone constantly and get feedback from the clients. Keep very close to the clients, too: it's about how they perceive the service of the firm. Talk to all employees, regardless of level, to make sure that the firm's culture is understood beyond just the top management team. I see some managing partners failing in this: they are maybe too introverted; maybe they have been promoted to their position because they are good organisers. But if you don't have this social skill, then I think you are doomed to fail.*

"Managing a law firm is a full-time role if you have more than 50 lawyers. I think many managing partners make this mistake. They love servicing clients, and they think they can make management a part-time role. But if you do that, you just end up dealing with administrative things and fire-fighting, and you never really get into strategic leadership."

You must lead by example. If you talk about a flat hierarchy or an informal leadership style, then show it. If you're talking about collaboration, then show what collaboration is and ensure that you don't have a remuneration system in the firm which disincentivises it, because that happens all too often. Lawyers by nature are cynical about the written word. Whatever you're trying to write is always interpreted and it is very difficult to make an impression on lawyers by writing. Lead by example.

Advice to a senior or managing partner

- It's a full-time role for a firm of 50 lawyers or more.
- Talk to everyone, all the time, both in-house and outside: in particular, talk to peers abroad as you will always learn from them.
- Lead by example.

Aku Sorainen
Founder and senior partner, Sorainen
aku.sorainen@sorainen.com

Sorainen is an international, integrated business law firm, with offices in the three Baltic States – Lithuania, Latvia and Estonia – and in Belarus. Founded in 1995, today the firm has 34 partners and over 200 lawyers and tax specialists.

Aku Sorainen is the founder and senior partner of Sorainen. Aku is of Finnish origin, but has worked as a lawyer in the Baltic States since 1993. He is specialised in M&A and real estate law and leads the firm's strategic development.

In 2015 Aku was honoured to receive the Knight's Cross, First Class, of the Order of the Lion of Finland from Finnish President Niinistö and in 2021 he was awarded the Service Cross of the Estonian Foreign Ministry for promoting Estonia's national interest. Aku is also the Honorary Consul of Malta in Estonia. He is recognised as an eminent practitioner in *Chambers Global.*

Linda Woolley

Managing partner, Kingsley Napley LLP

Linda Woolley is the managing partner of Kingsley Napley LLP, a London firm founded in 1937 and best known for its criminal law practice. Linda has managed the firm since 2007, overseeing the growth of the firm's income by 180%. Employing more than 200 lawyers, Kingsley Napley has been the highest-ranking law firm for the last three years in the *Sunday Times* 100 Best Companies to Work For.

Early years

Linda graduated from Warwick University in 1983 with a degree in English and American Literature. Her mother worked for their local council and Linda got a summer job in their PR department. She started to study marketing and communications, but it did not interest her, so she decided to try A level law to see if she liked it. She thought that law might be a good career because it touches on all aspects of life. It was either that or teaching; but her teacher friends had very low morale at the time, because of Margaret Thatcher's reforms, and when Linda got a grant from Essex County Council to study for the solicitors' exams, she thought she would try law first.

She lived at home while studying for the professional exams. When she got to law school, she realised that most of the other students had arranged articles and she had better get her act together. She thought she wanted to do criminal law and applied to firms with a general practice that included criminal. She was accepted by Kingsley Napley, which then gave her a grant to complete her studies. At her interview, they asked her why she wanted to be a lawyer:

> *I remember saying, "because I want to help people". Which is really kind of clichéd. But it is true, to be honest.*

Linda was impressed by the diversity of the firm's recruitment. One recruit was the son of a client, but another had an LLM from Oxford. Although Linda had no connections, she always felt at home:

> *We had an initial meeting. I met the other trainees – three or four others. And we were appointed to our seats, as in which team you would go to. I think there were only four teams in the firm. Some of the young solicitors took us out for lunch, or was it just a drink? We were in Covent Garden in those days, I was kind of fresh out of the 1980s PR world. And I was the only one who asked for alcohol. All the others were like – lemonade. And I'm thinking, OK... But I was always very comfortable and at home. The girl who had come out of Oxbridge, Jane, and I were sharing a room. So we had great fun, really. And we became very close friends. Jane and I are still friends now.*

Criminal law

Linda was impressed by the fact that in those days the firm did a lot of legally aided criminal work and treated its legal aid clients just as well as those who were paying the fees themselves. The firm had a "massive social commitment".

Linda was never going to be a corporate lawyer.

"I'm not the best lawyer in the room, in my opinion. Whenever David Napley asked for some research, my heart would sink because I'd always think someone else could do it better than me."

It's a strange thing for a managing partner to say, but I didn't really get it when I was at law school. And I didn't get property or trusts at all. I remember exchanging contracts on a property, and I put my contract into my drawer. I wasn't really thinking about the fact I had to send it somewhere. And then the guy rang me a couple of days later and said I still haven't received the contract.

I'm more interested in people and why they do things. Why they've found themselves in the situation they're in. And, you know, what do you do about it?

I'm not the best lawyer in the room, in my opinion. Whenever David Napley asked for some research, my heart would sink because I'd always think someone else could do it better than me. And I'm not really that interested in the construction of a phrase in a law statute, whether it means this or that, I couldn't be a barrister and disappear into the intricacies of legal construction. But I'm really interested in and like the fact that, for example, in criminal law, the law, including statute law, adapts and changes according to the morality of society at any time. So if you look at historic sexual abuse, child abuse, now, to a degree we are judging people, and not only judging them, but charging and convicting them on the basis of today's moral standards, rather than those of the time in which some of those acts were committed.

I've got reasonably good judgement around people. I'm very disciplined. I quite enjoy reading and studying. And I think because I started out in other work, which was much less interesting to me than the law, and where you have no control over what you're going to be doing that day, I couldn't believe my luck. I was doing criminal law in the best criminal practice in the country.

So I loved it. I think that gave me a real advantage. I mean, it has its stresses, but it's a great job.

Making a real difference

One case in particular stands out for Linda. She had a great success with a reinsurance fraud case, with the client acquitted at The Old Bailey in three hours after a nine-week trial, and two years later the barrister involved called Linda. A painter and decorator working at his house had asked him to look at some papers about his stepfather and the barrister asked Linda to help him on a *pro bono* basis.

It was a man who had been in prison for about nine or 10 years at that time for the murder of an old lady. And he said he hadn't done it. And the evidence was quite difficult. It was interesting. Anyway, I took it on and went to see him. The barrister and I both felt that his conviction was unsafe. We took various avenues. We were turned back and refused a couple of times by the Court of Appeal. And the barrister said, "OK, well, that's it". But this was just when the Criminal Cases Review Commission had come into being. And I said, "Well, I think we can take it to the CCRC". So we did. And they said, "No", and we threatened to judicially review them. And so they agreed to take it one further step. Anyway, very long story short, we got a hearing at the Criminal Court of Appeal which sits at the Royal Courts of Justice in London.

On the first day, the court tore our counsel to pieces. I had to comfort our client by saying that was "normal". Then we called an eminent pathologist who had given evidence for the Crown at the original trial including evidence about the time of death. We had evidence about the temperature on the day, and what happens to the stomach contents. We asked him whether, if he'd known what we were now putting before him, his evidence would have been different. There was a long pause. He said, "Yes, it would have been different". The judges withdrew and came back 15 minutes later, declared the conviction unsafe and quashed the conviction.

My client didn't even know what was happening. He didn't know what the decision meant for him, because it was all legalese. It was a classic scene. In the court used for criminal appeals they've got a dock area with bars. And I went up to him and explained that he was free and he kind of slipped down the bars. He was so shocked. He just kind of collapsed. And later we got him £750,000 in compensation.

And that is the only case in my whole life where, but for me, he probably would have died in prison. It stays with me, that case, because I know that I made the difference. And that is what my firm does for people every day, which is great.

The path to partnership

Linda was made a partner in the firm in 1998, after a client had told the firm she should be promoted. "It was very, very informal in those days." Linda became a salaried partner at first and the only difference it made was that she got a box of wine at Christmas and a free copy of the *Evening Standard* every night.

Linda was only the second woman to be made a partner at the firm in the criminal practice. Life continued much as before until she made a move to management in 2004. Until then, the firm had no real management structure. There were three joint managing partners, drawn from different parts of the firm – family, real estate and criminal. The three met with the finance director every Thursday and there was no change to their fee-earning responsibilities. By 2007, the others had withdrawn, leaving Linda as the sole managing partner.

The move to management

Linda says she is much more strategic than she used to be: "To be honest, I never used to fully understand what it meant." Now she says it means having a plan and an understanding of how to achieve your objectives. The plan for Kingsley Napley is to grow organically, focusing the growth particularly on the corporate, real estate and private client practices until they have greater critical mass and a stronger balance to the firm's traditional strengths in crime and litigation.

Did Linda enjoy the move to management?

I found it quite tough. A year in, once the shine had worn off, you'd worry that being managing partner was quite a poisoned chalice. Because you typically did it for three or six years, then you've lost your practice. I saw that some of my peers didn't have the support of the partners to regain their practice. And you're not a professional manager, either. So, you've got nowhere else to go. I became a bit anxious that this might have been a career-ending move. That was only me, no one was saying that I wasn't very good. That was just me worrying about it. And then I had a tough patch about three years ago. I think, because the firm was just getting too big for the model that I'd run the firm through. Then, with the

"I like being the decision maker. In the end, I'm the decision maker for almost everything we do. And I like that. And you know, we've done a lot of good things at the firm. And I'm proud of it."

support of our senior partner Stephen Parkinson, we created a management board. The first board meeting was in January 2019.

Before then, it was just me and an increasingly good management team of non-lawyers. I would find a line through to the full equity and the whole partnership, kind of keeping them in the loop of what we were doing next – the business plan and so forth, but in quite an informal way. And inevitably, as time goes on and the firm grows, more of the partners are not those who chose me to be managing partner in the first place. So you have to build a different relationship with them.

But I do really enjoy it. Probably about five years ago, it had been thought I would go back to be the head of criminal, but I didn't want to do that. I like being the decision maker. In the end, I'm the decision maker for almost everything we do. And I like that. And you know, we've done a lot of good things at the firm. And I'm proud of it, especially on the cultural side.

Kingsley Napley used to be called kind and nice, and it was both a positive and a term of derision. But now I think it's something we can be really proud of as well as it being good business. We've worked on what we stand for and what our brand stands for and we have evolved whilst still being true to our heritage. I have made a fair few tough decisions in my life, which involved parting company with people. When I was first managing partner, I stood up to some bullying – not of me personally – and some people left the firm who weren't kind and nice. And I'm proud of that. And I'm proud of the fact that we introduced values. When I became managing partner, businesses didn't really have values. And I think I would have been laughed at if I'd gone around with my little book of values. But we have introduced values and once you have them and embed them, they are a very good way of guiding your decision making.

Management theory – and practice

After she was appointed to manage the whole firm, Linda went on the short Harvard course on leading professional service firms. She took two points away with her, contrasting but "quite useful". The first was the importance of alignment – waiting until the circumstances are propitious – and the second was not to overlook the small things you can do in the meantime.

Linda thinks that management is both giving direction and offering a service, but giving direction first:

"I don't like the type of lawyer who thinks that business support teams are there just to support them. 'We pay for you', kind of thing. I think there's a danger that if you succeed in making lawyers' lives as easy as possible, you create that dynamic."

> *I always used to say to our heads of HR, BD & marketing and finance: It's our job to make the lawyers' lives as easy as possible. So, if we want them to do appraisals, make it easy for them to do them well. But I think you can cross the line there. I don't like the type of lawyer who thinks that business support teams are there just to support them. "We pay for you", kind of thing. I think there's a danger that if you succeed in making lawyers' lives as easy as possible, you create that dynamic. As firms become more professional you just can't survive now the way you could, when we were young lawyers: I didn't even know what IT was in those days. I think that successful firms will only continue to be successful when they treat their best managers as being on a par with them in terms of their contribution to the growth and success of the business. It's not all about the lawyers these days.*
>
> *In a way, it's a problem that we still insist on being managed by lawyers. I always thought that I would hand over to a CEO. I don't think that now – I don't think it would be the right thing. But when partners come over from the "other side" into management, typically, you can see a transformation in their respect for their colleagues in the business services side of the practice. And also the whole team in terms of what they provide, whereas when they're purely lawyers, or even practice area leaders, they think they're not quite commodities, but that you can get more of them where they came from. They don't realise how they're probably less indispensable than 90% of your lawyers. And so I think management of a law firm as well as leadership of it is really important.*
>
> *I think it's the people side, that's really, really vital. In a lot of law firms the managing partner will be a corporate lawyer, which is not a bad thing. But I think there needs to be somebody who really is into the people. And it's partly why I get on very well with our CFOO, who I brought in 10 years ago, because we complement each other; we don't want to cover the same territory. And that works really well, for both of us. We really respect each other. But we're not interested in the same bits of work.*

Linda thinks that her successor will probably be a lawyer:

> *I think there's something about lawyers only trusting other lawyers to know what it's like, and what their challenges and motivators are, and also what their stresses are, I guess. I think it gives you credibility and a bit more acceptance.*

Linda would like her partners to have a little more confidence. She says that lawyers take pride in being analytical and being risk averse is worn as a badge of honour.

I'm as risk averse as most people but, you know, you have to take chances, don't you, to try and get better, and be confident that you will succeed. I think sometimes lawyers are so cautious and so risk averse that it kind of holds us back.

Advice to a senior or managing partner

- Be decisive. Making a bad decision is usually better than not making a decision at all. As part of that, don't get too down about making mistakes – you must accept that you won't make the best decisions all the time.
- Listen, a lot.
- It is a good thing to be "nice and kind".

Linda Woolley
Managing partner, Kingsley Napley LLP
lwoolley@kingsleynapley.co.uk

Linda Woolley joined Kingsley Napley in 1990 as a trainee and qualified into the Commercial Litigation department in 1992, aged 30, before joining the Criminal department two years later. She became a partner in 1998. Linda continued to practise in criminal law, specialising in fraud and international crime, after she became a joint managing partner of the firm in 2004. She became the managing partner of Kingsley Napley in 2007.

Linda is a West Ham United season-ticket holder. She loves walking, theatre, ballet, opera and visiting art galleries.

© Stephanie Williams

About the editor

Bill Knight
Former senior partner, Simmons & Simmons
bill@knightsight.uk

Bill Knight worked for Simmons & Simmons for 35 years – from articled clerk to senior partner. Before he became senior partner he was in charge of the firm's Hong Kong Office and corporate department and chaired the Law Society's Company Law Committee. He is the author of *The Acquisition of Private Companies and Business Assets*, which ran to seven editions.

Since leaving the firm in 2001, Bill has been president of the City of London Law Society, deputy chairman of Lloyd's of London, chair of the Financial Reporting Review Panel and a gambling commissioner. He was a specialist adviser to the Treasury Select Committee on the enquiry into the failure of the Royal Bank of Scotland and in 2016 was awarded the OBE for services to financial regulation.

Bill is now a professional photographer, specialising in portraits, opera and the theatre, twice a winner in the "Portrait of Britain" photographic competition and with two portraits in the National Portrait Gallery. His website is www.knightsight.uk.

About Globe Law and Business

Globe Law and Business was established in 2005. From the very beginning, we set out to create law books which are sufficiently high level to be of real use to the experienced professional, yet still accessible and easy to navigate. Most of our authors are drawn from Magic Circle and other top commercial firms, both in the UK and internationally.

Our titles are carefully produced, with the utmost attention paid to editorial, design and production processes. We hope this results in high-quality publications that are easy to read and a pleasure to own. Our titles are also available as ebooks, which are compatible with most desktop, laptop and tablet devices. In 2018 we expanded our portfolio to include journals and Special Reports, available both digitally and in hard-copy format, and produced to the same high standards as our books.

We'd very much like to hear from you with your thoughts and ideas for improving what we offer. Please do feel free to email me at sian@globelawandbusiness.com with your views.

Sian O'Neill
Managing director
Globe Law and Business

www.globelawandbusiness.com